# NATIONS, CULTURES AND MARKETS

The Society for Applied Philosophy is concerned with the philosophical discussion of areas of practical concern, including environmental and medical ethics, the social implications of scientific and technical change, and philosophical and ethical issues in education, law and economics.

Membership enquiries to: The Honorary Secretary Ms Jane Pritchard, Centre for Professional Ethics, University of Central Lancashire, Preston PR1 2HE

# Nations, Cultures and Markets

*Edited by*

PAUL GILBERT

PAUL GREGORY

# Avebury

Aldershot · Brookfield USA · Hong Kong · Singapore · Sydney

Published by
Avebury
Ashgate Publishing Company
Gower House
Croft Road
Aldershot
Hants GU11 3HR

Ashgate Publishing Company
Old Post Road
Brookfield
Vermont 05036
USA

**British Library Cataloguing in Publication Data**

Nations, Cultures and Markets. (Avebury Series
 in Philosophy)
 I. Gilbert, Paul   II. Gregory, Paul
 III. Series
 155.89
 ISBN 1 85628 695 9


**Library of Congress Cataloging-in-Publication Data**

Nations, cultures and markets / edited by Paul Gilbert and
 Paul Gregory.
      p. cm. -- (Avebury series in philosophy)
 Rev. papers presented at the 1992 Conference of the Society for
 Applied Philosophy, held at the Isle of Thorns, Sussex.
 ISBN 1-85628-695-9 : $58.95  (approx.)
 1. International economic relations.  2.  International relations.
 3. Nationalism.  I. Gilbert, Paul, 1942–  .  II. Gregory, Paul.
 III. Society for Applied Philosophy.  Conference (1992 : Sussex,
 England)  IV. Series.
 HF1359.N38  1994
 337--dc20                                                        94-12100
                                                                      CIP

Typeset by Paul Gregory in Bodoni Book using Facelift for Wordperfect.

Printed and Bound in Great Britain by
Athenaeum Press Ltd, Newcastle upon Tyne.

# Contents

# Contributors and affiliations

**Chris Allen,** Centre For Economic Forecasting, London Business School, U.K.

**Harry Beran,** Department of Philosophy, The University of Wollongong, New South Wales, Australia

**Gordon Burt,** Institute of Educational Technology, Open University, U.K.

**Phillip Cole,** School of Philosophy and Religious Studies, Middlesex University, U.K.

**Michael Freeman,** Department of Government and Human Rights Centre, University of Essex, U.K.

**David George,** Department of Politics, University of Newcastle-Upon-Tyne, U.K.

**Paul Gilbert,** Department of Philosophy, University of Hull, U.K.

**David Gosling,** Daepartment of Educational Development, University of East London, U.K.

**Paul Gregory,** Hamburg, Germany

**Heta Häyry & Matti Häyry,** Department of Philosophy, University of Helsinki, Finland

**David Miller,** Nuffield College, Oxford, U.K.

**Bhikhu Parekh,** Department of Politics, University of Hull, U.K.

**Frances Woolley,** Department of Economics, Carleton University, Ontario, Canada

# Acknowledgements

The papers in this volume are revised versions of those given at the 1992 Conference of the Society for Applied Philosophy held at the Isle of Thorns, Sussex.

The editors are grateful in particular to David Miller and to the editors and publishers (Basil Blackwell Ltd.) of the Journal of Applied Philosophy for permission to republish his paper here, which formed the Conference Address. We are equally grateful to Hugo Wolfram for permission to publish the paper by Heta Häyry & Matti Häyry, which originally appeared in the International Journal of Moral and Social Studies under the editorship of the late Dr. Sybil Wolfram. Some minor linguistic changes have since been made to this paper.

Thanks are also due to Terry Oliver for his prompt and practical help in converting disks and files.

# 1 Nations, cultures and markets: An introduction

*Paul Gilbert*

## I

Recent years have witnessed an international paradox. On the one hand there has been an increasing globalisation of markets in commodities and products. Few countries of the world, if any, now operate largely self-sufficient economies. With the globalisation of markets has come, secondly, a correspondingly global culture. Coca Cola, it is trite to observe, is a rapidly acquired taste, a taste for Western fashions of consumption, appreciation, life style and thought. They are fashions which sweep away traditional cultures in those societies that take no steps to counter their influence. And those that do are viewed as singly unfriendly, defying the Enlightenment aspiration,

> That every distant land the wealth might share,
> Exchange their fruits and fill their treasures there;
> Their speech assimilate, their empires blend,
> And mutual interest fix the mutual friend.[1]

Thus, thirdly, there is an increasing globalisation of political control. Although the system of nation states remains largely unquestioned the political freedom of individual states is increasingly constrained by the threat of international intervention. Or, as critics might phrase it, western cultural imperialism heralds western imperialism: that is how "empires blend" in the contemporary world.

But against these trends run three opposing ones. First and most evident, is the rise of nationalisms which rupture larger systems of political control. The Russian Empire is no more and other federal structures have collapsed. Against this background critics of a closer European union arising from the Single European Act have muttered dire prognostications. Secondly, the liberal consensus which underpins the possibility of global culture has come under increasing attack. *Particular* cultures, by contrast, are held to be the sole

1

source of value, rather than simply systems of social behaviour and thought, of which the individual may make a rational evaluation and choice. Traditional cultures, then, become more closed and self-contained. Third, the globalisation of markets does not, except within well defined limits, extend to labour. Instead, there is increasing control of economic migration and an attendant identification of people, even in Europe, in terms not of their role in production, but of their place of origin. People seem on the way to becoming a country's only distinctive, but non-exportable, product.

How are we to understand these apparently contradictory phenomena? Or rather, since many kinds of understanding are required here, how *as philosophers* may we contribute to some understanding? We need to investigate our concepts of the nation, of its culture and of its way of life, and to tease out the relationships between them. We need to discover what ethical principals might regulate the relations between nations, between cultural groups and between economic players in the world market. And we need to do so not just as academic observers, but as participants in the political debates that involve these issues. We need to be, that is to say, not just philosophers but applied philosophers here. Each of the contributors to this volume undertakes one or more of these tasks, many of them with special reference to the issue of 1992 which occasioned their conference papers — the implications for nationhood, culture and market morality of greater European unity. But it had already become apparent that this was but one example of a wider global debate.


## II


There is an ideal conception which inextricably links communal identity, cultural values and economic role. It is an ideal with which other, more attenuated, conceptions of identity can be usefully compared. For though, in contemporary circumstances, it may be in practice quite unrealised, it is an ideal that continues to shape influential views of what is lost and visions of what might be restored. We find it allegorised in the middle of the last century in Christina Rossetti's mysterious *Goblin Market*:

> Morning and evening maids heard the goblins cry
> "Come buy our orchard fruits
> Come buy, come buy:
> Apples and quinces,
> Lemons and oranges...
> Figs to fill your mouth,
> Citrons from the south,
> Sweet to tongue and sound to eye;
> Come buy, come buy".[2]

Thus do the goblin merchant men attempt to seduce two very evidently English sisters, one of whom, Laura, muses wistfully,

> "How fair the vine must grow
> Whose grapes are so luscious,
> How warm the wind must blow
> Through those fruit bushes."

> "No" said Lizzie, "No, No, No,
> Their offers should not charm us,
> Their evil gifts would harm us."

As indeed they do harm Laura, who succumbs to them:

> She no more swept the house,
> Tended the fowls or cows,
> Fetched honey, kneaded cakes of wheat,
> Brought water from the brook.

The muscular rhythms of the verse here mimic the strenuous economic effort of the North by contrast with the languorous patterns of consumption in the South.

In the poem Laura's "dwindling" — her loss of identity, values and an economic role — is only arrested when her sister Lizzie confronts the goblins,

> Like a royal virgin town
> Topped with gilded dome and spire
> Close beleaguered by a fleet
> Mad to tug her standard down.

And, though they force their fruit upon her, she

> Would not open lip from lip
> Lest they should cram a mouthful in.
> But laughed in heart to feel the drip
> Of juice that syruped all her face.

So, when Laura kisses her,

> Her lips began to scorch,
> That juice was wormwood to her tongue,
> She loathed the feast.

To taste the fruit as *repudiated*, rather than to find it sweet, restores Laura to her culture and to life — to a life in which the sisters get married, have

3

children and celebrate the strength of family bonds "in calm or stormy weather".

*Goblin Market* is, in part, about identity, the kind of identity of which national identity is a species. It is identity as a member of a group living together in a particular locality which places constraints on what is a possible or desirable way of life for them. (The kernel-stone that Laura saves from the goblin fruits refuses to grow away from the soil that feeds "their hungry thirsty roots".) The members of the group are linked by ties of kinship or the opportunities of extending their kin, provided, for example, by regular marital relationships. They share a culture of common rules and values — "We must not look at goblin men, We must not buy their fruit" — in particular they share those rules and values that guide appreciation, govern patterns of consumption and regulate sexual activity (for which Laura's indulgence of her appetite is a metaphor). The culture reflects and reinforces the way of life founded upon the modes of production and consumption made possible by the place. It valorises what conduces to communal life there. There is for the community no viable alternative to that culture because its way of life is given, and for the individual no coherent alternative identity is possible.

In *Goblin Market* the identity thus presented is *English* identity. Ironically Christian Rossetti was three-quarters Italian. Her verse here conveys an *affirmation* of Englishness and a denial of Italian claims upon her[3] — an affirmation for which her own involuntarist conception of identity leaves no room. The Southern fruit merchants are irremediably alien, at best only *semi*-human "goblin men" with exotic animal characteristics, "Ratel- and wombat-like... Parrot-voiced and whistler." Englishness defines itself as what is fully human, and it does so because its values of orderliness, hard work, restraint and family commitment are taken to be definitively human values. The ready availability of food, or sex, is seen as dehumanising, animal. And the two go together, just as sexual restraint and economic reliance on family are together necessary for getting a living on northern soil.

The upshot of this picture is deeply xenophobic. Imported goods themselves and the market that makes them available are a threat to culture and thence to effective communal life. Their producer's culture is incomprehensible except as threatening, evil, and relations with them are miscegenative, unnatural. There is no possibility that people should be mutually enriched when they "exchange their fruits... their speech assimilate, their empires blend." National identities are comprehensive and exclusive. The integrated ideal which offers a complex and coherent identity to individuals threatens to result in racism, intolerance and dismal autarky. Any account of national identity — or, say, *European* identity — which relies on its appeal has to show how it can avoid these vices.

4

# III

One way to derive the advantages of the integrated ideal in the service of national identity, while apparently escaping its drawbacks, is to treat the picture of national life it generates as *mythic*. Images of life in an English farmhouse, for example, serve as a focus for a shared attachment to a place and its people; they record no facts about them. This we may call, without irreverence, the *sentimentalist* view of national identity, depending, as David Miller's paper makes clear, on the existence of common sentiments, rather than any factually common life, as what unites people in one nation. Kipling caught it well, a generation of imperialist expansion after Rossetti:

> Buy my English posies!
> Kent and Surrey may —
> Violets of the Undercliffe
> Wet with Channel spray.[4]

And so on cries the flower seller, as she hawks 'weeds ye trample underfoot' around the colonies:

> Far and far our homes are set round the Seven Seas
> Woe for us if we forget, we that hold by these!
> Unto each his mother-beach, bloom and bird and land —
> Masters of the Seven Seas, Oh, love and understand.

The colonists and those at home enjoy no obvious common life — the flowers, unlike Rossetti's fruit, lack any economic or seriously cultural significance — but they can imagine themselves as having a common life through the shared sentiments the flowers evoke (sentiments which, Kipling implies, those at home are in danger of losing).

The sentimentalist view provides for a national identity disconnected from other cultural identities, for example religious ones, and from actual economic roles. It is only successful, however, in forming a significant part of individual identity if it creates an illusion of shared culture and common life — of diverging values and interests sunk, that is to say, in a collective purpose. The purpose, it hardly needs adding, is a political one. And to the extent to which the illusion is successful there *is*, with respect to such limited purposes, a shared life and culture.

An account like this promises to avoid the ills of the integrated ideal. If national identity is founded on sentiment then there is no reason why anyone who can cultivate it should fail to qualify; and all that seems required for its cultivation is the shared soil of the national territory as a present or past abode. Racism is, theoretically, avoided, and so are cultural intolerance and economic insularity. For if national identity is mythic then, firstly, no particular way of life is essential to it and, secondly, one's own myths have no claim to superiority over others. The problem, of course, is that these points will be lost sight of to the extent to which the myth really does grip the imagination: racism, intolerance and insularity may be the consequence.

The sentimentalist view escapes this conclusion, it could be argued, only by construing national sentiments not as *beliefs*, which need factual reinforcement, but as *commitments* — voluntarily adopted attachments to a land and people. Yet this introduces a model of national identity quite at variance with what I have called the integrated ideal, and unable to rely on its resources for making national identity a significant part of individual identity. It is a *voluntarist* model in which national identity depends upon what oneself and others *choose* to be the group with which to associate politically. Voluntarism makes one's national identity depend, not on facts about one, whether of kinship, culture or common life, not even on facts about one's beliefs or wishes about those things, but upon these wishes themselves, on condition that others' wishes coincide with one's own. Then "the existence of a nation is" in Ernst Renan's much quoted phrase, "a daily plebiscite".

Voluntarism has two related drawbacks. First, it fails to provide one with any enduring reason for choosing to associate politically with those one does: that choice is entirely contingent, and not founded on any facts about them in virtue of which it is more proper to associate with some than with others. Yet not all principles of association, even within a common territory, one might suppose, give rise to national groups. Second, voluntarism fails to show how national identity can be a part of individual identity: who one already is, in terms of societal, cultural or economic role, may determine one's choice, but one's chosen national identity cannot determine who one is. One might think, however, that, for better or worse, one's nationality, like one's family, is something *given* in one's life, even if there are some limited opportunities for disowning it.

These drawbacks notwithstanding, voluntarism has great attractions, for it captures the universalist aspiration for a free exchange of goods, ideas and identities. Under voluntarism political associations are fluid because freely entered and regulated rationally on the basis that "mutual interest fix the mutual friend". Indeed the voluntarist account of national identity coheres together with an account of economic life as simply the upshot of individual economic choices, and of culture as the sum total of individual valuations manifest in society. Indeed it springs from a liberal individualism which values personal freedom above all else, since it discerns no criterion of value other than the satisfaction of individual desires whatever they may be. For all Rossetti's enunciation of a quite different ideal in her affirmation of English-ness, voluntarism gives rise, as Heta and Matti Häyry observe in their paper, to a recognisably *English* kind of nationalism.

What may be contrasted with that is German nationalism. We can see this as proposing an *ethnic* conception of a national identity which depends

6

precisely upon facts about people, rather than upon their wishes. These facts can be of various sorts — racial, linguistic, cultural, historical or whatever. The point is that they serve as evidence of really existing affinities and differences, so that it might strike one, as it struck Mazzini that "God divided humanity into distinct groups upon the face of our globe and thus planted the seeds of nations. Bad governments have disfigured the design of God".[5] Not all the factors I mentioned are evidence, we may note, of *natural* groupings. What is given is not necessarily natural; so if race is thought of as natural not all ethnic nationalisms are racist. Indeed racism can only gain the benefits of the integrated ideal if it derives a shared culture and life from a common inherited character. Ethnic nationalisms which found national identity directly upon shared culture are better placed. Yet common cultural values and common interests are distinct: culturalism has work to do to show how a common life that requires the latter is derivable solely from the former.

Can ethnic nationalism avoid the ills of xenophobia, intolerance and insularity? Conventional wisdom has it that it can so long, and only so long, as the boundaries of states are coincident with the boundaries of ethnic nations. For then aliens need pose no threat to a politically assured identity, and their products, cultural and economic, can be accepted or rejected on the nation's own terms without jeopardising its values and wellbeing. Border guards and customs posts are, on this picture strictly necessary to civilised international relations. It is a message heard recently in, for example, debates about the partition of Yugoslavia, which may well lead one to doubt at least its practicability.


## IV

When do national groups have a claim to independent statehood? In contrast to the ethnic response, Harry Beran gives the classic voluntarist answer: when they have a common will to statehood. He derives this answer from the liberal-democratic doctrine that "normal adults have the moral right of personal self-determination and, therefore, the moral right to determine their political relationships". David George argues, by way of qualification, that the democratic principle is not to be confused with the principle of national self-determination. The former is concerned with implementing the aggregate of individual wills; the latter with implementing people's corporate will as a nation. But this, he argues, presupposes that they already possess a corporate identity, and that is not something which can be accomplished merely by people willing it.

Indeed we do need to distinguish, like John Locke,[6] between people's agreement "to join and unite into a community for their comfortable, safe, and peaceable living, one amongst another, in a secure enjoyment of their properties, and a greater security against any that are not of it" from the resulting *community's* consent to obey a government — consent that a secessionist minority group might withhold. Locke's account of the formation of a political community appeals to a voluntary act of association — a social contract — between its members exercising, as Michael Freeman notes, their individual human rights. The nation so formed exists for the purpose of mutual protection. It is coextensive with a state or, if it is not, with a body which has, in relevant respects, a state-like organisation and which aspires to statehood.

It is precisely because its purposes *are* those of a state that the nation, conceived as a voluntary association, has a claim to independent statehood. It is formed for mutual protection and therefore has a claim to provide it. On liberal-democratic principles, this claim derives from the will of a majority in the community. But in a state from which a minority group wishes to secede there may be *two* political communities — that which is coextensive with the state, and that which is coextensive with its secessionist part. The will of the majority in the former gives its consent to the government, the will of the majority in the latter withholds it. Beran argues for a presumption in favour of the latter community's claim to statehood, George for a presumption in favour of the former's, when it more clearly has a corporate existence than the latter.

An alternative approach which seeks to circumvent this problem characterises political communities otherwise than as voluntary associations. Communitarianism, as Freeman and others term it, in contrast to liberalism, views the community as something *given*, rather than deliberately formed or entered; determining, rather than being determined by, our individual purposes; and held together by reciprocal relationships that are intrinsically valued, rather than by self-interested ones. It is, in Toennies' famous distinction, *Gemeinschaft* rather than *Gesellschaft*.[7] This, it may be argued, reveals the true character of the nation, which can thus be conceived of quite independently of the state which may represent it.

On this account national communities have, or at least can easily be treated as having, a corporate existence. Though there are no doubt many overlapping and nesting communities — families, clans, regional groups, trans-national groupings — nations are taken to have a specific form, in particular in the regulation of their member's behaviour by laws or law-like customary rules. The state is viewed as the organisation normally in practice needed to enforce these laws. *Independent* statehood is, it is argued, required to safeguard the laws against changes which threaten the distinctness of the community, and, perhaps, *self-government* to prevent sectional interests jeopardising its solidarity. Communitarianism thus provides a prima facie case for self-determination, though the assumption that there are clearly discernible *national* communities is questionable. Precisely the same competing claims may arise as under liberal-democratic theory. But now it appears to be a question of *fact* which claim is to be preferred, depending upon which is the community whose rules are both most overarching and most deeply internalised (even if sometimes this question will yield no determinate answer).

The communitarian nations' claim to statehood is only as good, it may be objected, as is the particular way of life which statehood preserves. It may be replied that under communitarianism there is no neutral extra-communal standpoint from which to evaluate the life of the community. Yet here we must be careful. The communitarian's claim is not a claim on behalf of a *culture*, any more than a claim to respect a *family's* identity and independence, within limits, is a claim on behalf of its particular ethos and manners. A culture, unlike a community, is something which can be expressed in individual behaviour and can be regarded as a benefit to individuals independent of membership of a community. Indeed possession of a common culture does not yet constitute joint membership of any community, since it does not form individuals into a collective whole. Conversely a distinct community need have no distinctive culture, its culture may change, yet its value for its members may lie in the *particular* attachments it involves, which are unavailable to others, as in a family. From within a community, as from within a family, however, we can appreciate the value that such attachments can have, even if we cannot share them.

This distinction between community and culture is an important one. Ethnic nationalism can sustain a prima facie claim to statehood only to the extent to which it represents a suitable community. By no means all ethnic nationalisms aim to make this case. We can, broadly speaking, distinguish those that locate national identity in participation in a network of relationships (as does the integrated ideal) from those that locate it in properties of the individual members — racial, cultural or whatever. The latter, non-communitarian ethnic nationalism, has to rely on arguments for statehood from the value of distinctive characters and cultures in individual motivation or social cohesion. But now a *special* case needs making out that something worthwhile would be endangered without an independent state set up to preserve it.

## V

What is a distinctive culture and what is its value anyway? T. S. Eliot, comparing it with religion, characterised it as "the whole way of life of a people".[8] It includes, he went on, "all the characteristic activities and interests of a people" and listed:

> Derby Day, Henley Regatta, Cowes, the Twelfth of August, a Cup Final, the dog races, the pin table, the dart board, Wensleydale cheese, boiled cabbage cut into sections, beetroot in vinegar, Nineteenth Century Gothic Churches and the music of Elgar.

9

While some (e.g. Bhikhu Parekh) are sceptical of the value of a culture so constructed, others (e.g. Paul Gregory) see it as an essential part of the narrative framework of people's lives. Both take culture to be a way of life *as understood and valued* by its participants, not as something describable in terms other than their own. This distinction leaves room for discrepancies between people's culture and their life. On the one hand a culture might express a quite distorted conception of actual social life; on the other actual social life might distort a worthwhile culture. There are competing requirements upon culture here: while it is not possible to understand one's life *except* as culturally conceived, culture should make real understanding *possible*. The first calls for cultural richness and coherence, the second for flexibility and openness. It may well be doubted whether in the context of contemporary nations the latter demand is likely to be met.

David Gosling raises a similar doubt about the founding of a *European* identity in shared myths of the sort Miller regards as necessary to national identity. He believes it threatens both pluralism within Europe and openness to those outside the community. But whether it does depends, presumably, on the precise nature of the myth: some are more restrictive than others. The Irish nationalist George Russell wrote:

> We hold the Ireland in the heart
> More than the land our eyes have seen,
> And love the goal for which we start
> More than the tale of what has been...
> No blazoned banner we unfold —
> One charge alone we give to youth,
> Against the sceptred myth to hold
> The golden heresy of truth.[9]

There is however a *myth* here, but a principally prospective rather than retrospective one, a myth in which, in de Valera's version, what had been dreamed of would be the home of a people who valued material wealth only as the basis of a right living, of a people who were satisfied with frugal comfort and devoted their leisure to the things of the spirit .[10] That myth failed in Ireland. The culturally restrictive last splendour of the Gael is, as Russell feared, more potent there. But this is not to say that a country or region *cannot* have the resources for a myth that fosters both solidarity and openness. In its heyday the universalist myth of liberalism did that for Europe, creating, as Derrida astutely notes[11] a paradox for contemporary European identity as it spreads beyond Europe's territorial bounds.

As Rossetti saw, nothing threatens a particular culture as much as an extension of the market. Gregory and Gordon Burt both discuss this process, the latter through a systems approach. Conversely Gosling and Phillip Cole both demonstrate how entry into economic life carries with it no necessary cultural integration:

> Here's hands so full o' money an' hearts so full o' care,
> By the luck o' love! I'd still go light for all I did go bare.
> "God save ye, *Colleen dhas*," I said: the girl she thought me wild[12]

laments an Irish worker in England, sexual rejection epitomising, as always, cultural exclusion. It is, of course, a relation of exploitation, not reciprocity, raising a particular form of the question to what degree communities are justified in partiality towards their existing members. This is a question which arises more generally in relation to whether economic arrangements can be just if they benefit the community at the expense of those outside it.

Chris Allen & Frances Woolley investigate the welfare gains and losses of the Single European Market, concluding that it will have an adverse effect on less developed countries. They and Gosling question whether this can be just. A tension arises here between the economic liberalism which holds that a free market is necessary to secure equal opportunities for a good life and the communitarianism which asserts that market relations cannot conduce to the community which is necessary for it. Yet it is not a principle of community life in general, only of particular communities, that they should pursue their own economic interests at peril of abandoning "a right living". Arguably it is the liberalism which has shaped European life that yields unjust consequences, not a belated gesture in the direction of communitarianism.

Indeed it could be argued that just as communitarianism requires relations of reciprocity between members so it demands respect for, and fair treatment of, other communities; for if the life of the community is valuable to us then it is valuable to others too, and we can have no right to deprive others of the conditions for such a life when we already possess them ourselves. The counter to this argument is to claim that it is solely a community organised in accordance with the *right* values which gives rise to a valuable life. But this is again to give precedence to a particular culture over the general benefits of community. It is this that is incompatible with pluralism and liberality, not a thoroughgoing communitarianism.


## VI

We return, then, to the point from which we started: can national or transnational identity provide a cultural significance and value to shared economic activity and geographical experience, yet avoid the ills of racism, intolerance and closure? Or should we settle for the attenuated and unstable identity of voluntarism? In any case we have little opportunity for choice here, even if we knew how to choose. We can hope, at best, to gain some understanding of current developments, to favour some and to fear others as they tend for good

11

or ill.

A communitarian approach to national or to trans-national identity does not by itself, I have suggested, have either tendency: that depends on the character of the community. I have also demurred at the view that its moral character is not something which can be assessed except in terms of the community's own particular culture. There are, I would claim, general principles which determine whether a community works well or ill, independent of its attendant culture. Such a culture may give a distortedly favourable impression of bad workings or serve to damage good ones. This is, of course, only to make the old point that culture involves ideological processes which may operate to the advantage of some sections of the community rather than to that of the community as a whole. For the latter the community as a whole must, so far as is possible, control its own way of life. But this requires a culture that provides for a critical understanding of social life, and which is open to consensual change.

Undoubtedly not all cultures do provide for this. In particular many foster a conception of national identity which is radically at odds with the social and economic realities to which it should be referable. If community consists in a day to day willingness to live together in relations of reciprocity then it is often present where people's explicit political wishes are for separation and exclusion (and sometimes absent when for union and integration). People can be just wrong as to the facts relevant to claims for separate (or for common) statehood. These errors may well affect voting in plebiscites, and it is this which gives rise to the greatest dangers of voluntarism.

Ethnic or cultural affiliations are, in general, no *disqualification* to community membership, while an appropriate economic role is a positive qualification for it. Racism and intolerance can have no necessary place in sustaining a working community, though they can and do serve to bolster cultures which disguise the lack of one, as, notoriously, under Fascism. The integrated ideal is possible, in other words, only if it is *genuinely* integrated, as many existing national identities are not.

All of this concerns what is *in principle* a possibility. Whether it is so in practice and, more especially whether it is so in conditions of a globalised market economy, is another question. *Goblin Market* depicts an extension of just such market relations into an environment regulated by communal ones. The community is threatened and reacts by a policy of exclusion. Whether communities can in practice survive otherwise under these conditions (if indeed national statehood itself can any longer guarantee such a policy against international interference) must remain an open question. The contribution that philosophy can make here is not to answer it, but, as itself a component of our culture, to explore and perhaps extend the cultural resources available for tackling this situation in which we find ourselves.

12

# Notes

1.  Joel Barlow, quoted David Simpson "Destiny made manifest" in Homi K. Bhabha (ed): *Nation and Narration* (Routledge, 1990).
2.  *Goblin Market and Other Poems* (1862).
3.  See "Italia lo Ti Saluto" in *A Pageant and other Poems* (1881).
4.  "The Flowers" in *The Seven Seas* (1896).
5.  *The Duties of Man* (Dent 1907) p. 52.
6.  *Second Treatise on Civil Government* (1690) Section 95.
7.  *On Sociology: Pure, Applied and Empirical* (University of Chicago Press, 1971) p. 131 ff.
8.  *Notes towards the Definition of Culture* (Faber 1962) p.31.
9.  "On Behalf of Some Irishmen Not Followers of Tradition", *Collected Poems*, (1913).
10. Quoted D. G. Boyce: *Nationalism in Ireland* (Croom Helm, 1982) p. 351.
11. *The Other Heading* (Indiana University Press 1992).
12. Moira O'Neill, "Corrymeela" in *Songs from the Glens of Antrim* (1900).

# 2 In defence of nationality[1]

*David Miller*

My story begins on the river bank of Kenneth Grahame's imagination.

> "And beyond the Wild Wood again?" [asked the Mole]: "Where
> it's all blue and dim, and one sees what may be hills or perhaps
> they mayn't, and something like the smoke of towns, or is it only
> cloud drift?"

> "Beyond the Wild Wood comes the Wide World," [said the Rat].
> "And that's something that doesn't matter, either to you or me.
> I've never been there, and I'm never going, nor you either, if
> you've got any sense at all. Don't ever refer to it again, please."[2]

The Rat, so very sound in his opinions about most things, boats especially,
seems in this moment to reveal exactly what so many people find distasteful
about national loyalties and identities. He displays no overt hostility to foreign
lands and their ways. But the combination of wilful ignorance about places
beyond the Wild Wood, and complete indifference to what is going on there,
seems particularly provoking. Aggressive nationalism of the "my country right
or wrong" variety is something we might at least argue with. But the narrowing
of horizons, the contraction of the universe of experience to the river bank itself,
seems to amount to the triumph of sentiment over reasoned argument.

Philosophers, especially, will have great difficulty in coming to grips with the
kind of national attachments for which I am using the Rat's riverbankism as an
emblem. Philosophers are committed to forms of reasoning, to concepts and
arguments, that are universal in form. "What's so special about this river
bank?" a philosophical Mole might have asked in reply. "Why is this river
bank a better place than other river banks beyond the Wood?" To which the
Rat could only have said. "This is my place; I like it here; I have no need to
ask such questions."

The Rat, clearly, is no philosopher. Yet in contemplating his frame of mind

15

we might be led to recall the words of one who was:

> ...there are in England, in particular, many honest gentlemen, who
> being always employ'd in their domestic affairs, or amusing
> themselves in common recreations, have carried their thoughts little
> beyond those objects, which are every day expos'd to their senses.
> And indeed, of such as these I do not pretend to make philo-
> sophers....They do well to keep themselves in their present
> situation; and instead of refining themselves into philosophers, I
> wish we cou'd communicate to our founders of systems, a share of
> this gross earthy mixture, as an ingredient, which they commonly
> stand much in need of, and which wou'd serve to temper those
> fiery particles, of which they are composed.[3]

Plainly the Rat is well supplied with gross earthy mixture, literally and
metaphorically, and the question is whether any philosophical system can make
use of what he has to offer. The sort that can is the Humean sort. By this I
mean a philosophy which, rather than dismissing ordinary beliefs and sentiments
out of hand unless they can be shown to have a rational foundation, leaves them
in place until strong arguments are produced for rejecting them. The Rat's
beliefs cannot be deduced from some universally accepted premise; but that is
no reason for rejecting them unless the arguments for doing so seem better
founded than the beliefs themselves. In moral and political philosophy, in
particular, we build upon existing sentiments and judgements, correcting them
only when they are inconsistent or plainly flawed in some other way. We don't
aspire to some universal and rational foundation such as Kant tried to provide
with the categorical imperative.

It is from this sort of stance (which I shall not try to justify) that it makes
sense to mount a philosophical defence of nationality. There can be no question
of trying to give rationally compelling reasons for people to have national
attachments and allegiances. What we can do is to start from the premise that
people generally do exhibit such attachments and allegiances, and then try to
build a political philosophy which incorporates them. In particular we can do
two things: we can examine the critical arguments directed against nationality
— arguments trying to undermine the validity of national loyalties — and show
that they are flawed; and we can try to assuage the tension between the ethical
particularism implied by such commitments and ethical universalism, by
showing why it may be advantageous, from a universal point of view, that people
have national loyalties.[4]

Philosophers may protest that it is a caricature of their position to suggest that
the only reasons for belief or action that they will permit to count are those that
derive from an entirely impersonal and universal stand-point. It is common now
to distinguish between agent-neutral and agent-relative reasons and to give each
some weight in practical reasoning. But what motivates this concession is

16

mainly a concern for individuals' private goals and for their integrity: people must be given the moral space, as it were, to pursue their own projects, to honour their commitments, to live up to their personal ideals. National allegiances, and the obligations that spring from them, are harder to fit into this picture, because they appear to represent, not a different segment of moral life, but a competing way of understanding the concepts and principles that make up the impartial or agent-neutral stand-point (consider, for example, the different conceptions of distributive justice that emerge depending on whether you begin from a national or a universal starting-point). That is why such loyalties appear to pose a head-on challenge to a view of morality that is dominant in our culture, as Alasdair MacIntyre has argued.

It is a curious paradox of our time that while nationalism is politically on the advance, its would-be defenders (in the West at least) find themselves on the defensive. I have just given one reason for this: the view that national allegiances cannot withstand critical scrutiny, so a rational person cannot be a nationalist. There is also a more mundane reason: nationality is widely felt to be a backward-looking, reactionary notion; it is felt to stand in the way of progress. In the European context, for instance, we are invited to look forward to a "Europe of the regions" in which Catalonia, Brittany, Bavaria, Scotland and the rest co-exist harmoniously under a common administrative umbrella, free from the national rivalries which have plunged us into two world wars. Progress means the overcoming of nationality. In the Oxford branch of the Body Shop (and doubtless in the branches in Paris, Tokyo, and elsewhere) you can buy a lapel badge that quotes H. G. Wells: "Our true nationality is mankind." H. G. Wells and the Body Shop in tandem epitomise the modern idea of progress, whose disciples were described by George Orwell in such a wonderfully acid way: "all that dreary tribe of high-minded women and sandal-wearers and bearded fruit-juice drinkers who come flocking towards the smell of "progress" like bluebottles to a dead cat". If you are one of these bluebottles, and most of us are to some degree, then you will think that ordinary national loyalties amount to reactionary nostalgia and queue up to sport the H.G. Wells slogan.

So the would-be nationalist has two challenges to meet: the philosophical challenge and the progressive challenge. And now it is time to spell out more precisely the notion of nationality that I want to defend. Nationality as I shall understand it comprises three interconnected propositions. The first concerns personal identity, and claims that it may properly be part of someone's identity that they belong to this or that national grouping; in other words that if a person is invited to specify those elements that are essential to his identity, that make him the person that he is, it is in order to refer to nationality. A person who in answer to the question "Who are you?" says "I am Swedish" or "I am Italian" (and doubtless much more besides) is not saying something that is irrelevant or bizarre in the same way as, say, someone who claims without good evidence that he is the illegitimate grandchild of Tsar Nicholas II. Note that

17

the claim is a permissive one: national identity may, but need not, be a constitutive part of personal identity.

The second proposition is ethical, and claims that nations are ethical communities. They are contour lines in the ethical landscape. The duties we owe to our fellow-nationals are different from, and more extensive than, the duties we owe to human beings as such. This is not to say that we owe *no* duties to humans as such; nor is it to deny that there may be other, perhaps smaller and more intense, communities to whose members we owe duties that are more stringent still than those we owe to Britons, Swedes, etc at large. But it is to claim that a proper account of ethics should give weight to national boundaries, and that in particular there is no objection in principle to institutional schemes that are designed to deliver benefits exclusively to those who fall within the same boundaries as ourselves.

The third proposition is political, and states that people who form a national community in a particular territory have a good claim to political self-determination; there ought to be put in place an institutional structure that enables them to decide collectively matters that concern primarily their own community. Notice that I have phrased this cautiously, and have not asserted that the institution must be that of a sovereign state. Historically the sovereign state has been the main vehicle through which claims to national self-determination have been realised, and this is not just an accident. Nevertheless national self-determination *can* be realised in other ways, and as we shall see there are cases where it must be realised other than through a sovereign state, precisely to meet the equally good claims of other nationalities.

I want to stress that the three propositions I have outlined — about personal identity, about bounded duties and about political self-determination — are linked together in such a way that it is difficult to feel the force of any one of them without acknowledging the others. It is not hard to see how a common identity can support both the idea of the nation as an ethical community and the claim to self-determination, but what is more subtle — and I shall try to bring this out as I go along — is the way in which the political claim can reinforce both the claim about identity and the ethical claim. The fact that the community in question is either actually or potentially self-determining strengthens its claims on us both as a source of identity and as a source of obligation. This interlinking of propositions may at times seem circular; and the fact that the nationalist case cannot be spelt out in neat linear form may confirm philosophical suspicions about it. But I believe that if we are to understand the power of nationality as an idea in the modern world — the appeal of national identity to the modern self — we must try to understand its inner logic.

So let me now begin to look more closely at national identities themselves, and in particular ask what differentiates them from other identities — individual or communal — that people may have. What does it mean to think of oneself as

18

belonging to a national community?

The first point to note, and it has been noted by most of those who have thought seriously about the subject, is that national communities are constituted by belief: a nationality exists when its members believe that it does. It is not a question of a group of people sharing some common attribute such as race or language. These features do not of themselves make nations, and only become important insofar as a particular nationality takes as one of its defining features that it members speak French or have black skins. This becomes clear as soon as one looks at the candidates that have been put forward as objective criteria of nationhood, as Ernest Renan did in his famous lecture on the subject: to every criterion that has been proposed there are clear empirical counter-examples. The conclusion one quickly reaches is that a nation is in Renan's memorable phrase "a daily plebiscite"; its existence depends on a shared belief that its members belong together, and a shared wish to continue their life in common. So in asserting a national identity, I assume that my beliefs and commitments are mirrored by those who I take to share that identity, and of course I might be wrong about this. In itself this does not distinguish nationality from other kinds of human relationship that depend on reciprocal belief.

The second feature of nationality is that it is an identity that embodies historical continuity. Nations stretch backwards into the past, and indeed in most cases their origins are conveniently lost in the mists of time. In the course of this history various significant events have occurred, and we can identify with the actual people who acted at those moments, reappropriating their deeds as our own. Often these events involve military victories and defeats: we imagine ourselves filling the breach at Harfleur or reading the signal hoisted at Trafalgar. Renan thinks that historical tragedies matter more than historical glories. I am inclined to see in this an understandable French bias, but the point he connects to it is a good one: "sorrows have greater value than victories; for they impose duties and demand common effort". The historic national community is a community of obligation. Because our forebears have toiled and spilt their blood to build and defend the nation, we who are born into it inherit an obligation to continue their work, which we discharge partly towards our contemporaries and partly towards our descendants. The historical community stretches forward into the future too. This then means that when we speak of the nation as an ethical community, we have in mind not merely the kind of community that exists between a group of contemporaries who practise mutual aid among themselves and which would dissolve at the point at which that practice ceased; but a community which, because it stretches back and forward across the generations, is not one that the present generation can renounce. Here we begin to see something of the depth of national communities which may not be shared by other more immediate forms of association.

The third distinguishing aspect of national identity is that it is an active identity. Nations are communities that do things together, take decisions, achieve results, and so forth. Of course this cannot be literally so: we rely on proxies who are seen as embodying the national will: statesmen, soldiers, sportsmen, etc. But this means that the link between past and future that I noted a moment ago is not merely a causal link. The nation becomes what it does by the decisions that it takes — some of which we may now regard as thoroughly bad, a cause of national shame. Whether this active identity is a valuable aspect of nationality, or whether as some critics would allege merely a damaging fantasy, it clearly does mark out nations from other kinds of grouping, for instance churches or religious sects whose identity is essentially a passive one insofar as the church is seen as responding to the promptings of God. The group's purpose is not to do or decide things, but to interpret as best it can the messages and commands of an external source.

The fourth aspect of a national identity is that it connects a group of people to a particular geographical place, and here again there is a clear contrast with most other group identities that people affirm, such as ethnic or religious identities. These often have sacred sites or places of origin, but it is not an essential part of having the identity that you should permanently occupy that place. If you are a good Muslim you should make a pilgrimage to Mecca at least once, but you need not set up house there. A nation, in contrast, must have a homeland. This may of course be a source of great difficulties, a point I shall return to when considering objections to the idea of nationality, but it also helps to explain why a national community must be (in aspiration if not yet in fact) a political community. We have seen already that nations are groups that act; we see now that their actions must include that of controlling a chunk of the earth's surface. It is this territorial element that makes nations uniquely suited to serve as the basis of states, since a state by definition must exercise its authority over a geographical area.

Finally it is essential to national identity that the people who compose the nation are believed to share certain traits that mark them off from other peoples. It is incompatible with nationality to think of the members of the nation as people who merely happen to have been thrown together in one place and forced to share a common fate, in the way that the occupants of a lifeboat, say, have been accidentally thrown together. National divisions must be natural ones; they must correspond to real differences between peoples. This need not, fortunately, imply racism or the idea that the group is constituted by biological descent. The common traits can be cultural in character: they can consist in shared values, shared tastes or sensibilities. So immigration need not pose problems, provided only that the immigrants take on the essential elements of national character. Indeed it has proved possible in some instances to regard immigration as itself a formative experience, calling forth qualities of resourcefulness and mutual aid that then define the national character — I am thinking of the settler cultures of the New World such as the American and the Australian. As everyone knows, there is nothing more illustrious for an

Australian today than to have an ancestor who was carried over in chains by the First Fleet.

When I say that national differences must be natural ones, I mean that the people who compose a nation must believe that there is something distinctive about themselves that marks them off from other nations, over and above the fact of sharing common institutions. This need not be one specific trait or quality, but a range of characteristics which are generally shared by the members of nation A and serve to differentiate them from outsiders. In popular belief these differences may be exaggerated. Hume remarked that the vulgar think that everyone who belongs to a nation displays its distinctive traits, whereas "men of sense" allow for exceptions; nevertheless aggregate differences undoubtedly exist. This is surely correct. It is also worth noting that people may be hard pressed to say explicitly what the national character of their people consists in, and yet have an intuitive sense when confronted with foreigners of where the differences lie. National identities can remain unarticulated, and yet still exercise a pervasive influence on people's behaviour.

These five elements together — a community constituted by mutual belief, extended in history, active in character, connected to a particular territory, and thought to be marked off from other communities by its members' distinct traits — serve to distinguish nationality from other collective sources of personal identity. I shall come in a moment to some reasons why such identities may be thought to be particularly valuable, worth protecting and fostering, but first I should emphasize what has so far merely been implicit, namely the mythical aspects of national identity. Nations almost unavoidably depend on beliefs about themselves that do not stand up well to impartial scrutiny. Renan once again hit the nail on the head when he said that "to forget and — I will venture to say — to get one's history wrong, are essential factors in the making of a nation". One main reason for this is that the contingencies of power politics have always played a large part in the formation of national units. States have been created by force, and, over time, their subject peoples have come to think of themselves as co-nationals. But no-one wants to think of himself as roped together to a set of people merely because the territorial ambitions of some dynastic lord in the thirteenth century ran thus far and no further. Nor indeed is this the right way to think about the matter, because the effect of the ruler's conquests may have been, over time, to have produced a people with real cultural unity. But because of the historical dimension of the nation, together with the idea that each nation has its own distinct character, it is uncomfortable to be reminded of the forced nature of one's national genesis. Hence various stories have been concocted about the primeval tribe from which the modern nation sprang. The problem is, of course, particularly acute in the case of states created relatively recently as a result of colonial withdrawal, where it is only too obviously the case that the boundaries that have been drawn reflect the vagaries of imperial competition. It is easy for academic critics to mock the

21

attempts made by the leaders of these states to instil a sense of common nationhood in their people. I myself recall, when teaching in Nigeria in the mid-1970s, reading with some amusement earnest newspaper articles on the question whether the country did or did not need a national ideology — it seeming obvious that a national ideology was not something you could just decide to adopt.

The real question, however, is not whether national identities embody elements of myth, but whether they perform such valuable functions that our attitude, as philosophers, should be one of acquiescence if not positive endorsement. And here I want to argue that nationality answers one of the most pressing needs of the modern world, namely how to maintain solidarity among the populations of states that are large and anonymous, such that their citizens cannot possibly enjoy the kind of community that relies on kinship or face-to-face interaction. That we need such solidarity is something that I intend to take for granted here. I assume that in societies in which economic markets play a central role, there is a strong tendency towards social atomisation, where each person looks out for the interests of herself and her immediate social network. As a result it is potentially difficult to mobilize people to provide collective goods, it is difficult to get them to agree to practices of redistribution from which they are not likely personally to benefit, and so forth. These problems can be avoided only where there exists large-scale solidarity, such that people feel themselves to be members of an overarching community, and to have social duties to act for the common good of that community, to help out other members when they are in need, etc.

Nationality is *de facto* the main source of such solidarity. In view of the broadly Humean approach that I am adopting, where our moral and political philosophy bends to accommodate pre-existing sentiments, this in itself would be enough to commend it. But I should like to say something more positive about nationality before coming to the difficulties. It is precisely because of the mythical or imaginary elements in national identity that it can be reshaped to meet new challenges and new needs. We have seen that the story a nation tells itself about its past is a selective one. Depending on the character of contemporary politics, the story may gradually alter, and with it our understanding of the substance of national identity. This need not take the crude form of the rewriting of history as practised in the late Soviet Union and elsewhere (airbrushing pictures of Trotsky out of the Bolshevik central committee and so on.) It may instead be a matter of looking at established facts in a new way. Consider, as just one example, the very different interpretation of British imperialism now current to that which prevailed at the time of my father's birth in Edwardian Britain. The tone has changed from one of triumphalism to one of equivocation or even mild apology. And this goes naturally along with a new interpretation of British identity in which it is no longer part of that identity to shoulder the white man's burden and carry enlightenment to the heathen.

From a political stand-point, this imaginary aspect of nationality may be a source of strength. It allows people of different political persuasions to share a political loyalty, defining themselves against a common background whose outlines are not precise, and which therefore lends itself to competing interpretations. It also shows us why nationality is not a conservative idea. A moment's glance at the historical record shows that nationalist ideas have as often been associated with liberal and socialist programmes as with programmes of the right. In their first appearance, they were often associated with liberal demands for representative government put forward in opposition to established ruling elites. Linda Colley's studies of the emergence of British nationalism in the late 18th and early 19th centuries show that nationalist ideas were developed by middle class and popular movements seeking to win a place in the public realm, and resisted by the state and the landowning class that supported it. This picture was repeated in its essentials throughout Europe. It is easy to see why a conservative may resist nationalism. Nationality invokes the activist idea of a people collectively determining its own destiny, and this is anathema to the conservative view of politics as a limited activity best left in the hands of an elite who have been educated to rule. Two of the most swingeing of recent attacks on nationalism have come from acolytes of Michael Oakeshott, Elie Kedourie and Kenneth Minogue. Minogue regards nationalism as essentially a revolutionary theory and "therefore a direct enemy of conservative politics". He offers a reductive psychological explanation of its appeal: "Nationalist theories may thus be understood as distortions of reality which allow men to cope with situations which they might otherwise find unbearable".

Nationality, then, is associated with no particular social programme: the flexible content of national identity allows parties of different colours to present their programmes as the true continuation of the national tradition and the true reflection of national character. At the same time it binds these parties together and makes space for the idea of loyal opposition, an individual or faction who resist prevailing policy but who can legitimately claim to speak for the same community as the government of the day. But its activist idea of politics as the expression of national will does set it against conservatism of the Oakeshott-Kedourie-Minogue variety.

I have referred to the liberal origins of the idea of nationality, but the first objection that I want to consider amounts essentially to a liberal critique of nationality. This holds that nationality is detrimental to the cultural pluralism that liberals hold dear; it is incompatible with the idea of a society in which different cultural traditions are accorded equal respect, and whose vitality springs from competition and exchange between these traditions. The classic statement of this critique can be found in Lord Acton's essay on "Nationality" in which he argues in favour of a multi-national state in which no one nation holds a dominant place. Such a state, he claims, provides the best guarantee

23

of liberties, "the fullest security for the preservation of local customs" and the best incentive to intellectual progress.

This argument derives from the assumption that national identities are exclusive in their nature; that where a state embodies a single nationality, the culture that makes up that nationality must drive out everything else. There is no reason to hold this assumption. Nationality is not of its nature an all-embracing identity. It need not extend to all the cultural attributes that a person might display. So one can avow a national identity and also have attachments to several more specific cultural groups: to ethnic groups, religious groups, work-based associations and so on and so forth. A line can be drawn between the beliefs and qualities that make up nationality, and those that fall outside its scope. The place where the line is drawn will be specific to a particular nationality at a particular time, and it will be a subject for debate whether its present position is appropriate or not. For instance one may argue in a liberal direction that a person's religion, say, should be irrelevant to their membership of this nation, or argue in a nationalist direction that language is not irrelevant, that each member should at least be fluent in the national tongue. The Acton argument supposes that no such line can be drawn. It supposes, contrary to all evidence, that one cannot have a pluralist society in which many ethnic, religious etc groups co-exist but with an overarching national identity in common.

Indeed one can turn Acton's argument around, as J. S. Mill did by anticipation in his chapter on Nationality in Representative Government. Unless the several groups that compose a society have the mutual sympathy and trust that stems from a common nationality, it will be virtually impossible to have free institutions. There will, for instance be no common interest in stemming the excesses of government; politics becomes a zero-sum game in which each group can hope to gain by the exploitation of the others.

This was Mill's argument, and there is plenty of subsequent evidence to back it up. But I want now to consider a more subtle variation on the theme that nationality and liberalism are at odds. This concedes that national identity and group identity can be kept separate, but points to the fact that national identities are always in practice biased in favour of the dominant cultural group, the group that historically has dominated the politics of the state. The state may be liberal in the sense that it does not suppress minority groups, but it does not accord equal respect and equal treatment to cultural minorities. Practical examples of this would include what is prescribed in the curricula in state-run schools, the content of what is broadcast through the national media, and so forth. The national identity includes elements drawn from the dominant culture, this is reproduced politically through the state, and minority groups are put at a disadvantage both in various practical respects and in the less tangible sense that their cultures are devalued by public neglect.

Concrete versions of this critique will be familiar to most readers. I want to

24

reply to it first by conceding that it is descriptively true in many historical cases — national identities have very often been formed by taking over elements from the group culture that happens to be dominant in a particular state — but then adding that it is not integral to national identities that they should be loaded in this way. I have stressed the malleability of nationality already, and one thing we may be doing in the course of redefining what it means to be British, French, etc is to purge these identities of elements that necessarily entail the exclusion of minority groups. Here there is one particular aspect of nationality that needs underlining. Although in standard cases a national identity is something one is born into — and I have argued that this factor of historical continuity is a source of strength — there is no reason why others should not acquire it by adoption. In this respect it contrasts with ethnic identities which generally speaking can only be acquired by birth. Although a priori a nation might define itself tightly by descent, in practice nations extend membership more or less freely to those who are resident and show willingness to exhibit those traits that make up national character. So although this does impose certain constraints on them, minority groups, particularly those migrating to the society in question, have the option of acquiring a new identity alongside their existing ones. Nationality, precisely because it aims to be an *inclusive* identity, can incorporate sub-groups in this way without demanding that they forsake everything they already hold dear.

Indeed one can take this further and say that what best meets the needs of minority groups is a clear and distinct national identity which stands over and above the specific cultural traits of all the groups in the society in question. The argument here has been well put by Tariq Modood, who has particularly in mind the position of Muslims in British society. He writes:

> As a matter of fact the greatest psychological and political need for clarity about a common framework and national symbols comes from the minorities. For clarity about what makes us willingly bound into a single country relieves the pressure on minorities, especially new minorities whose presence within the country is not fully accepted, to have to conform in all areas of social life, or in arbitrarily chosen areas, in order to rebut the charge of disloyalty. It is the absence of comprehensively respected national symbols in Britain, comparable to the constitution and the flag in America, that allows politicians unsympathetic to minorities to demand that they demonstrate loyalty by doing x or y or z, like supporting the national cricket team in Norman Tebbit's famous example.

To make my position clear here, I do not suppose that the superimposition of national identity on group identity that I am arguing for can be wholly painless on either side. While national identities are thinned down to make them more acceptable to minority groups, these groups themselves must abandon values and

25

ways of behaving that are in stark conflict with those of the community as a whole. National identity cannot be wholly symbolic; it must embody substantive norms. This will be readily apparent if a formal constitution occupies a central place in such an identity, as I believe it should. Forms of belief and behaviour inconsistent with those laid down in the constitution will be ruled out. So, as I have argued elsewhere, one cannot aspire to unlimited tolerance in this area. But the view I am defending does appear consistent with the kind of politically sensitive liberalism exhibited by J. S. Mill.

This, I hope, sufficiently addresses the liberal objection to nationality. Now I want to come to a second objection which might be termed the Balkan objection. This claims that the principle of nationality cannot in practice be realised, but meanwhile the belief that it can leads to endless political instability and bloodshed. This is because would-be nationalities are so entangled with one another that there is no way of drawing state boundaries that can possibly satisfy all claims. Minority group B secedes from state A in search of national self-determination, but this only provokes group C within B to attempt secession in its turn and so on *ad infinitum*. I call this the Balkan objection because of a view one frequently hears expressed nowadays that so long as the peoples of that region were governed from afar by the Austro-Hungarian and Turkish empires, different ethnic groups lived and worked happily side-by-side, but once those empires were weakened and the idea of national self-determination was let loose, impossible conflicts were generated. Recent events in Yugoslavia seem to confirm the view, and any day now I expect to hear President Tito's reputation being salvaged on the same terms as that of Emperor Franz Joseph.

The principle of nationality as formulated earlier holds that people who form a national community in a particular territory have a good claim to political self-determination. This principle should not be confused with a certain liberal view of the state which makes individual consent a necessary and sufficient condition of a state's authority. If each person must consent to the existence of the state, it follows that the borders of states should be drawn wherever people want them to be drawn. The practical implication is that any sub-community in any state has the right to secede from that state provided that it is in turn willing to allow any sub-sub-community the equivalent right and so on indefinitely. This view confronts the Balkan problem in its most acute form: where populations are intermingled, consistent application of the consent principle points directly towards an anarchic outcome in which no stable frontiers can be established.

The principle of nationality is quite different from this. Central to the idea of nationality is not individual will, but individual identity, even though some formulations confuse these two — Renan's idea of the nation as "a daily plebiscite" which I cited earlier is *in this respect* misleading. When we encounter a group or community dissatisfied with current political arrangements the question to ask is not "Does this group now want to secede from the existing state?" but "Does the group have a collective identity which is or has become incompatible with the national identity of the majority in the state?" There are broadly three answers that might be given to this question. First it may turn out that the dissatisfied group is an ethnic group which feels that materially speaking it is not getting a fair deal from the existing set-up and/or that its group identity is not being properly respected in national life. Black Americans would exemplify this: what is needed in such cases is domestic political reform, perhaps of a quite radical and painful kind, not dreams of secession. Second, the group may have a national identity, but one that is not radically incompatible with the identity of the majority community, there being common elements as well as elements of difference. The dissenting group thinks of itself as sharing a common historical identity with the majority, but also as having its own distinct national character which is currently not recognized. This may (I say this with some trepidation) represent the position of the Scots and Welsh in Britain, or the Bretons in France, and the appropriate outcome is again not outright secession (which violates the shared identity) but a constitutional arrangement which gives the sub-community rights of self-determination in those areas of decision which are especially central to its own sense of nationhood.

Finally there are cases where the state as presently constituted contains two or more nations with radically incompatible identities. The reason for this might be that one community takes as constitutive of its identity some feature such as language or race not shared with the others, or that its historical self--understanding includes military conquest of the territory now occupied by the second community, or some other such factor. In these cases there is no realistic possibility of formulating a shared identity, and the minority group has a prima case for secession. But to make the case a conclusive one, further conditions must be met. First, there has to be some way of redrawing the borders such that two viable states are created and this in itself may pose insoluble problems. Second, the territory claimed by the seceding community should not contain minorities whose own identity is radically incompatible with the new majority's, so that rather than creating a genuine nation-state, the secession would simply reproduce a multi-national arrangement on a smaller scale. Third, some consideration must be given to small groups who may be left behind in the rump state; it may be that the effect of secession is to destroy a political balance and leave these groups in a very weak position. It is, for instance, a strong argument against the secession of Quebec from the Canadian federation that it would effectively destroy the double-sided identity that Canada has laboured to achieve, and leave French-speaking communities in other provinces isolated and politically helpless.

What I am trying to stress is that the principle of nationality does not generate an unlimited right of secession. What it says is that national self-determination is a good thing, and that states and their constitutions should be arranged so that each nation is as far as possible able to secure its common future. Since

27

homogeneous nation-states are not everywhere feasible, often this will require second-best solutions, where each nationality gets partial self-determination, not full rights of sovereignty. Equally, there may be cases where communities are intertwined in such a way that no form of national self-determination is realistically possible, and the best that can be hoped for is a modus vivendi between the communities, perhaps with a constitutional settlement guaranteed by external powers.

That, somewhat elliptically, is my answer to the Balkan objection. The final objection I want to consider arises from the second aspect of the idea of nationality, the claim that nations are ethical communities. It runs as follows. You say that nations are ethically significant, that the duties we owe to fellow-members are greater in scope than those we owe to outsiders. You ground this in a shared sense of identity which is based not upon concrete practices but upon sentimental ties, on historical understandings which you have conceded to be imaginary in part. But how can duties of justice, especially, depend in this way on our feelings about others? Does this not make justice an entirely subjective idea, and abandon its role as a critical notion which serves to correct both our beliefs and our behaviour?

Observe to begin with that our sense of national identity serves to mark out the universe of persons to whom special duties are owed; it may do this without at the same time determining the content of those duties. In particular my recognition of X as a co-national to whom I have obligations may depend upon a sense of nationality with sentimental content, but it does not follow that my duties to X depend on my feelings about X as a person. An analogy with the family makes this clear. A family does not exist as such unless its members have certain feelings towards one another, yet obligations within the family are not governed by sentiment. I may feel more sympathy for one child than another, yet in allocating the family's resources I ought to consider their needs impartially.

It appears nonetheless that obligations in this account are being derived from the existence of a certain kind of community, while in the national case the community is sentiment-based. It would follow that if nation A embodies a strong sense of fellow-feeling whereas nation B embodies a relatively weak sense, then obligations within A are more extensive than those within B, and this seems paradoxical. What this overlooks, however, is the role played by political culture within national identity. It is not merely that I feel bound to a group of people defined in national terms; I feel bound to them as sharing in a certain way of life, expressed in the public culture. The content of my obligations stems immediately from that culture. Various interpretations of the public culture are possible, but some of these will be closer to getting it right than others, and this also shows to what extent debates about social justice are resolvable. It follows that what social justice consists in will vary from place to place, but not directly in line with sentiments or feelings. A Swede will acknowledge more extensive obligations to provide welfare for fellow-Swedes than an American will for fellow-Americans; but this is because the public culture of Sweden, defining in part what it means to be Swedish, is solidaristic, whereas the public culture of the U.S. is individualistic. It is not part of the story that Swedes must have more sympathetic feelings for other individual Swedes than Americans do for other Americans.

This may still sound an uncomfortably relativistic view to some. What I have argued is that nationalists are not committed to the kind of crude subjectivism which says that your communal obligations are whatever you feel them to be. Membership of a national community involves identifying with a public culture that is external to each of us taken individually; and although we may argue with one another about how the culture should be understood, and what practical obligations stem from it, this is still a question to which better or worse answers can be given.

Philosophers may find it restricting that they have to conduct their arguments about justice with reference to national identities at all. My claim is that unless they do they will lose contact entirely with the beliefs of the people they seek to address; they must try to incorporate some of Hume's gross earthy mixture, the unreflective beliefs of everyday life. Nonetheless there is a tension here. We should return to Kenneth Grahame's Rat who on his first appearance seems to stand for unlimited acquiescence in the everyday world of the river bank. As the story draws towards its conclusion, however, a more troubled Rat emerges. Disturbed first by the departure of the swallows to Southern climes, he then encounters a seafaring Rat who regales him with tales of the colourful and vibrant world beyond the river bank. The Rat is mesmerised. His eyes, normally "clear and dark and brown" turn to "a streaked and shifting grey". He is about to set out for the South with stick and satchel in hand, and has to be physically restrained by the Mole, who gradually leads his thoughts back to the everyday world, and finally leaves him writing poetry as a kind of sublimation of his wandering instincts.

The Rat's earlier refusal to contemplate the Wide World, it emerges, was a wilful repression of a part of himself that it was dangerous to acknowledge. Something of the same dilemma confronts the philosophical nationalist. He feels the pull of national loyalties, and he senses that without these loyalties we would be cast adrift in a region of great moral uncertainty. Yet he is also alive to the limitations and absurdities of his and other national identities. He recognises that we owe something to other human beings merely as such, and so he strains towards a more rationally defensible foundation for ethics and politics. There is no solution here but to strive for some kind of equilibrium between the everyday and the philosophical, between common belief and rational belief, between the river bank and the Wide World. But, as the cases both of the Rat and of David Hume in their different ways demonstrate, this is far easier said than done.

# Notes

1.    An earlier version of this paper was read to the Nuffield Political Theory Workshop and to the Society for Applied Philosophy's annual meeting at the Isle of Thorns, Sussex, and I should like to thank both audiences for their helpful comments. I am especially grateful to Jerry Cohen, Tariq Modood and Andrew Williams for discussion of some of the issues it addresses.

2.    K. Grahame, *The Wind in the Willows* (London, Methuen, 1926), pp. 16-17.

3.    D. Hume, *A Treatise of Human Nature*, ed. L.A. Selby-Bigge, 3rd edn revised P. H. Nidditch (Oxford, Clarendon Press, 1978), p. 272.

4.    I have attempted the second especially in "The Ethical Significance of Nationality", Ethics, 98 (1987-8), pp 647-62. I am mainly concerned with the first in the present paper.

5.    See for instance T. Nagel, *Equality and Partiality* (New York and Oxford, Oxford University Press, 1991) whose organizing idea is the contrast between personal and impersonal ethical standpoints.

6.    A. MacIntyre, "Is Patriotism a Virtue?" (Lawrence, University of Kansas, Department of Philosophy, 1984).

7.    G. Orwell, *The Road to Wigan Pier* (Harmondsworth, Penguin, 1962), p. 160.

8.    I speak of "nationality" rather than "nationalism" because the latter term usually carries with it unwelcome assumptions about what nations are entitled to do to advance their interests; however there is no alternative to "nationalist" as an adjective. An alternative approach would be to follow Neil MacCormick in distinguishing different conceptions of nationalism; like MacCormick's, the conception I want to defend includes the condition that in supporting my nation's interests, I should respect others' national identities (and the claims that follow from them) as well. See N. MacCormick, "Nation and Nationalism" in *Legal Right and Social Democracy* (Oxford, Clarendon Press, 1982) and N. MacCormick, "Is Nationalism Philosophically Credible?" in W Twining (ed.), *Issues of Self-Determination* (Aberdeen, Aberdeen University Press, 1991)

9.    E. Renan, "What is a Nation?" in A. Zimmern (ed.), *Modern Political Doctrines* (London, Oxford University Press, 1939).

10.   Ibid, p. 203.

11.   D. Hume, "Of National Characters" in *Essays Moral, Political, and Literary*, ed. E. Miller (Indianapolis, Liberty Classics, 1985), pp. 197-8.

12.   "It is only when you meet someone of a different culture from yourself that you begin to realize what your own beliefs really are." (Orwell, *Wigan Pier*, p. 145.)

13.  Renan, "What is a Nation?", p. 190.
14.  I should make it clear that this consideration could not be put forward as a reason for having or adopting a national identity. A national identity depends upon a prereflective sense that one belongs within a certain historic group, and it would be absurd to propose to the subjects of state X that because things would go better for them if they adopted a shared national identity, they should therefore conjure one up. The argument points to benefits that national allegiances bring with them as by- -products. Others who have defended nationality in this way include B. Barry, "Self-Government Revisited" in D. Miller and L. Siedentop (eds.), *The Nature of Political Theory* (Oxford, Clarendon Press, 1983), reprinted in B. Barry, *Democracy, Power and Justice* (Oxford, Clarendon Press, 1989); and Nagel, *Equality and Partiality*, ch. 15.
15.  I have argued this with specific reference to socialism in "In What Sense Must Socialism Be Communitarian?", *Social Philosophy and Policy*, 6 (1988-9), 51-73; but I believe the point holds more generally.
16.  See especially L. Colley, "Whose Nation? Class and National Consciousness in Britain 1750-1830", *Past and Present*, 113 (1986), 97-117.
17.  See E. J. Hobsbawm, *Nations and Nationalism since 1780* (Cambridge, Cambridge University Press, 1990).
18.  It is also true, however, that conservatives of a different persuasion may embrace national identities as a source of social cohesion and authority; see in particular R. Scruton, "In Defence of the Nation" in *The Philosopher on Dover Beach* (Manchester, Carcanet, 1990). I hope on another occasion to look more closely at what distinguishes this kind of conservative nationalism from other forms of communitarianism.
19.  E. Kedourie, Nationalism (London, Hutchinson, 1966); K. Minogue, *Nationalism* (London, Batsford, 1967).
20.  Minogue, *Nationalism*, p. 148
21.  There is a fine and suitably controversial example of this in Margaret Thatcher's recent attempt to present her political views as the logical outcome of British history and national character.

> I always said and believed that the British character is quite different from the characters of people on the Continent — quite different. There is a great sense of fairness and equity in the British people, a great sense of individuality and initiative. They don't like being pushed around. How else did this really rather small people, from the times of Elizabeth on, go out in the larger world and have such an influence upon it?...
>
> I set out to destroy socialism because I felt it was at

odds with the character of the people. We were the first country in the world to roll back the frontiers of socialism, then roll forward the frontiers of freedom. We reclaimed our heritage...

(M. Thatcher, "Don't Undo My Work", Newsweek, Vol 119, No. 17, April 27 1992, p. 14)

22. Lord Acton, "Nationality" in *The History of Freedom and other essays*, ed J. N. Figgis (London, Macmillan, 1907).

23. T. Modood, "Ethno-Religious Minorities, Secularism and the British State" forthcoming in T. Murphy (ed.), *Religious Freedom in Plural Societies*.

24. D. Miller, "Socialism and Toleration" in S. Mendus (ed.), *Justifying Toleration* (Cambridge, Cambridge University Press, 1988); *Market, State and Community*, ch.11.

25. One can find it expressed, for example, in Kedourie, *Nationalism*, chs 6-7.

26. See, for instance, H. Beran, "A Liberal Theory of Secession", *Political Studies*, 32(1984), 21-31 — though Beran would deny the consequence I wish to infer from this doctrine.

27. If this is allowed, it follows that there can be no simple answer to the question "How many nations are there in area A?". Nations are not discrete and easily counted entities like billiard balls. The criteria that I have offered to define them admit of degree, and that is why it is possible to have a smaller nationality nesting within a larger one.

28. The conditions given are intended to be necessary rather than sufficient. I have addressed the issue of justified secession at greater length in "The Nation-State: A Modest Defence" in C. Brown (ed.), *Political Restructuring in Europe — East and West: Ethical Perspectives* (London, Routledge, 1993).

# 3 Reason or nation? Two types of nationalism in today's Europe

*Heta Häyry and Matti Häyry*

European nationalism has historically assumed two main forms. The first form emphasizes individual rights, the supremacy of reason, and liberty from archaic traditions and oppressive social structures. This type of nationalism emerged in England during the seventeenth century, and its spirit animated the American and French Revolutions. The second main version originated in Germany in the eighteenth century. This form stresses the priority of instinct over reason, tradition over rational reform, and historical differences between nations over their similarities and common aspirations. The second type of ideology has always been readily identified as nationalist, and it has been at the core of many patriotic movements over the last two centuries. It is the first version, however, that has more often been presented under the allegedly universalistic labels of "liberalism" and "democracy".[1]

Our aim here is to show that the English type of nationalism is as real and originally as nation-centred as the German version of the creed. Both forms of the doctrine have their sources in elevated patriotic feelings, and the proponents of both creeds have evoked concepts like "blood" and "soil", "fatherland" and "mother tongue" to support their ideologies. Both forms of the doctrine have been employed to justify international aggression, expansionist policies, oppression and warfare. And both forms have been instrumental in justifiable as well as in unjustifiable nationalist movements.

If our view concerning the two types of nationalism is correct, then the prevailing tendency towards European economic unification may, in its present form, prove to be hazardous. If nations and cultures are seen, as they are at the present frequently seen, as dispensable obstacles to the free market, and if economic factors are allowed to dictate the content of political decisions, the reaction may be the rise of German-type nationalism in various parts of Europe. This, in its turn, could lead to a polarization, which would gradually increase the possibility of violent confrontation between the German-type and the English-type nationalist ideals. If political decision-makers wish to avoid this

33

result, they ought to begin to take both these forms of nationalism seriously before it is too late. A compromise which rejects the dangerous elements of both forms of nationalism but recognizes the sound and valuable elements in both would, we shall suggest, be the correct answer to the impending problems of European cooperation.

It should be noted that by using the terms "English nationalism" and "German nationalism" we do not mean to imply that England and Germany are the only European countries where patriotic feelings prevail. As our definitions will show, both ideologies can be found in any part of the world, often simultaneously. It should also be noted that there are, of course, many other types of nationalism besides the two that we have mentioned, both in Europe and in other continents. For our purposes in this paper, however, the division of nationalisms into the "English" and "German" types is sufficient.

## What is nationalism?

Some English readers will feel inclined to object at this point and to argue that, first, there is no such thing as "English nationalism", and, second, that even if there is, the doctrine cannot be linked with democracy and liberalism. From the viewpoint of British English the objection does in fact have some linguistic support. According to a typical concise British definition, nationalism means:

> patriotic feeling or principles or efforts; policy of national independence. (*The Pocket Oxford* 1984, s.v. *nationalism*.)

If this definition, or one resembling it, is accepted, it does not seem reasonable to postulate a link between nationalism and the ideals of liberty and democracy. Patriotic and isolationist policies are not usually known for their liberal or democratic zeal. This point is stated more explicitly in the *Encyclopaedia Britannica*, where nationalism is characterized as:

> the creed of those who believe that fidelity to one's state is of more importance than fidelity to international principles or to individual interests. (*The New Encyclopaedia* 1989a, 552.)

Devotion to one's nation or state, as opposed to a commitment to the advancement of one's personal aims or universalistic principles like liberty and democracy, seems to be one of the most prominent features of nationalism in British language and thought.

Devotion to one's nation as the core idea of nationalism is also emphasized in, for instance, French and Italian dictionaries. Thus the French word *nationalisme* is defined as follows:

> 1. The exaltation of national sentiment; the passionate attachment

34

to one's nation, sometimes accompanied by xenophobia and isolationism. ... 2. The doctrine founded on this sentiment, according to which all domestic politics should be subordinated to the development of the power of the nation, and according to which it is the nation's right to affirm to the outside world this power without limitations of sovereignty. ... 3. A doctrine or political movement which centres on a nationality's claim to form a nation-state.[2]

Likewise, the Italian *nazionalismo* is defined as the "political doctrine founded on the principle of nationality",[3] and the key word "nationality", or *nazionalità*, in its turn, is defined as the:

> principle according to which every nation has the right to turn itself into an independent state.[4]

These definitions, like their British counterparts, define nationalism primarily as the creed which, based on patriotic feeling, advocates the independence, sovereignty and self-rule of European-type nation-states.

The concept of nationalism implied by the American English usage deviates slightly but recognizably from the pattern set by the British English, French and Italian dictionaries. *Webster's*, for instance, defines nationalism thus:

> [Loyalty] and devotion to a nation; *esp*: a sense of national consciousness exalting one nation above all others and placing primary emphasis on promotion of its culture and interests as opposed to those of other nations and supranational groups. (*Webster's Ninth New* 1983, s.v. *nationalism*.)

According to another American dictionary, nationalism means, among other things:

> 1. national spirit or aspirations. 2. devotion to the interests of one's own nation. 3. desire for national advancement and independence. (*The Random House* 1968, s.v. *nationalism*.)

The distinctive feature of these definitions is that they do not confine the expressions of national feeling to attempts to gain national independence. Nationalists can also consider it their duty to promote the interests of their country by increasing its influence in other countries.

German definitions of nationalism take up, spell out, comment on and extend the point made by American English lexicographers. The idea of national expansion is not only included in German dictionaries but also explicitly criticized. This is how one German lexicon defines the word:

> *Nationalism*, the excessive, aggressive form of *national conscious-ness*, which developed ... during the French Revolution. National-

ism was a constructive force in the formation of European nation-states in the 19th and the early 20th centuries, but it also led to the one-sided and unscrupulous defence of egoistic national interests, accompanied by feelings of contempt towards the vitality of other nationalities and towards their right to survive. National-ism is based on the mistaken belief that those who cultivate and respect their own tradition must necessarily despise and oppose the traditions of other people.[5]

A more balanced but equally critical account of nationalism is given by a German encyclopaedia:

> *Nationalism*, the ideology which militantly, and both internally and externally, represents the thought of the nation and the (nation-)state that is based on it. Historically, culturally, ethnically, politically and socio-economically nationalism is a many-sided phenomenon, which may include the absolutization of national interests and hopes, contempt towards other nationalities and national minorities, and the connection of national consciousness (or national feeling) with elitism, evangelism or racism. These characteristics do not always appear simultaneously, or with equal intensity. Nationalism can be advocated by a distinct class of people, or by the whole nation. Nationalist armed forces aim internally at integration (assimilation, unity) by violence and externally at aggressive expansion. The nationalism of a national-ity may challenge the nationalism of another nationality, and thus create a potential conflict situation.[6]

Both German definitions emphasize the aggressive and expansive nature of nationalism, as opposed to the isolationism implied by the British English understanding of the term. If the American and German interpretations are preferred to the British, French and Italian readings, the connection between English nationalism and liberalism becomes less difficult to grasp.

## "English" nationalism and "German" nationalism

English nationalism in its original form was born as an offshoot of the seventeenth-century Puritan revolution, which stressed the importance of individual liberty and rational reform. These ideals in themselves were not, of course, exclusively British, but due to the political and religious upheavals of the era, it was easy for the British to see their country as the cradle of liberty and liberation. John Milton in a famous vision saw Britain as the centre from which the idea of freedom can be seen to spread to all corners of the earth. He

36

wrote:

> Surrounded by congregated multitudes, I now imagine that ... I behold the nations of the earth recovering that liberty which they so long had lost; and that the people of this island are ... disseminating the blessings of civilization and freedom among cities, kingdoms and nations. (*The New Encyclopaedia* 1989b, 469.)

In this vision England was seen as the "soil most genial to the growth of liberty" and the English people were seen as the reborn people of ancient Israel.

The original religious tone of English nationalism was not long-lived. The rise of the doctrine coincided with the rise of the mercantile middle classes in England, and the initial patriotism had to give way to the idea, encapsulated by John Locke (1690), that all individuals should be equally free regardless of national divisions. During the eighteenth century this variant of English nationalism spread to North America and was employed by the colonials against the mother country in the Revolution. The American Declaration of Independence was the first major political document which emphasized the liberal and humanitarian ideals of liberty, equality, and universal happiness.[7]

The eighteenth century also saw the transference of English-type nationalism to the European continent. In France, however, the ideals of liberty and equality were conditioned by Jean-Jacques Rousseau's (1762) potentially totalitarian doctrine of general national will. The core idea of the doctrine was that we, as individuals, are truly free only if "each of us puts his person and all his power in common under the supreme direction of the general will" (Rousseau 1762, 192). It is perhaps not surprising that the French Revolution, with its appeals to liberty, equality and fraternity (the last replacing individual happiness in the formula) soon found itself duplicating the oppressive political structures against which it had been originally directed. When individual freedom is subordinated to the general good, even democratic policies lose their fundamental liberal tendency.

The paradigm for the second type of European national feeling, German nationalism, emerged as an indirect result of the French Revolution. Napoleon with his citizen army created great havoc in Europe, and ideological reactions were inevitable. German intellectuals, who linked Napoleon's conquests with the ideals of the French Revolution, began to defend instinct against reason, and historical tradition against human-made attempts to create a more just social order. The principles of liberty and equality were seen as mere ideological disguises for French expansionism, and were rejected in favour of the rhetorically more appealing ideas of blood, soil and the heritage of past generations. In the 1930s the German National Socialist movement combined these ideas with racist agitation and totalitarian policies, and the practical results of that experiment are widely regarded as a refutation of all forms of German nationalism.

37

All German or German-type versions of nationalism cannot, however, be condemned simply because Hitler and his followers employed the central concepts of the doctrine for their own purposes. There are two good reasons for withholding reproof. First, the applications of the competing view, English-type nationalism, have not always been universally laudable themselves. In fact, it can be argued that supposedly liberal expansionist and colonial policies have in many cases been the source of radical German-type reactions. The "liberal" winners of the First World War, for instance, were not altogether innocent with regard to the rise of Fascism and Nazism in continental Europe. Second, despite the reference to murky notions like "blood" and "soil", German nationalism cannot be reduced to the racist pan-German ideals of the Third Reich. At the core of the doctrine is a potentially non-aggressive form of patriotism, which demands only cultural self-determination for each individual nation. This fundamental claim cannot be dismissed as easily as the illegitimate demands of interwar Germany and Italy.

Let us examine in more detail these two points which upset the customary value judgements attached to the two types of national self-expression.

As regards the darker side of spreading the gospel of liberty, the first, and perhaps historically the most important, misapplication of English nationalism was the creation of the British Empire. Attracted both by the riches of other continents and by the idea of spreading freedom among barbaric nations, England during the seventeenth and eighteenth centuries became one of the leading colonial powers. The consequences of that policy are still felt in many parts of the Third World. There are other instances of dangerous English-type nationalism. The Napoleonic wars extended the disadvantages of perverted democratic ideals to the European continent. The American form of misguided liberalism, in its turn, gave birth to a nation which suffers, from time to time, from grandiose and disastrous illusions of world domination. The Vietnam war was a case in point. And another self-styled saviour of the world was created in Eastern Europe in the Russian Revolution. While the Americans fight for democracy in the interest of multinational corporations, the proclaimed aim of the Soviet Union was to liberate all nations and classes from social alienation and economic oppression.

In all these cases it is clear that liberalism in and by itself could not have produced all the evil consequences which have followed from expansionism, and which have been effected in the name of universal freedom. But this is precisely what we wanted to prove. Nationalism, "English" or "German", cannot be conclusively condemned because of the historical misapplication of its sound basic principles. The suffering inflicted by imperialist policies cannot be blamed on the ideals of individual freedom and democracy. Nor can the suffering produced by the Nazis be blamed on the demand for cultural and political autonomy for each nation.

The fundamental principles of German and German-type nationalism were first

38

expressed in philosophical terms by Johann Gottfried von Herder in his book *Outlines of a Philosophy of the History of Man* (1784-91).[8] Herder took up the Kantian idea that "pure reason" is a myth, and that human intellect is always regulated by the *a priori* intuitions of time and space. According to Kant's view, the intuitions presupposed by experience are shared by all human beings regardless of historical or geographical divisions. But Herder argued that the way individual human beings perceive, think and act depends primarily on their nationality. Human beings are not basically citizens of the world, but members of more restricted groups, which have their own customs, life styles and cultural lives. The Kantian intuition of time was, accordingly, replaced in Herder's doctrine by the bulk of collective experience which is shared by the members of a national group, and the intuition of space was superseded by the sense of belonging to one's native land. Put together, these elements make up the *Volksgeist*, or national spirit, of a nation.

In his account of the history of humankind Herder drew a parallel between nations and living organisms. Each nation develops, or "grows", according to its own internal laws, which are determined by history and geography. Furthermore, if the life of a nation is interfered with, the consequences can be as disastrous as the consequences of uprooting a delicate plant. Violations of the cultural and political autonomy of a nation can easily drain its vitality, and if the drainage is severe, the nation withers away and dies, leaving individuals adrift. The abstract universalist concepts of reason and individual rights are, in Herder's opinion, a poor substitute for the sense of uniqueness and belonging that a nation can provide to its citizens.[9]

## The pros and cons of "English" and "German" nationalism

It seems, then, that both forms of European nationalism are based on reasonable claims which can, however, be employed to justify suspect domestic and foreign policies. The positive and negative sides of the "English" and "German" types of nationalism are sketched in Figure 1.

The positive elements of both forms of European nationalism are related to demands for freedom and security, but there are important differences between the creeds as regards the role of individuals within the nation or state. English-type nationalism stresses personal freedom both as a means to political stability and as an end in itself. Only individuals who are endowed with liberties and rights can establish and enforce a social structure which is both effective and just. On the other hand, one of the good features of an effective and just social structure is that it guarantees the personal freedom of each citizen and their right to pursue happiness. German-type nationalism, in its turn, holds that only the autonomy and self-determination of the nation can provide citizens with what is most important to them, namely security and a firm sense of belonging to a

39

|  | English Nationalism | German Nationalism |
| --- | --- | --- |
| Aspects which are generally regarded as *positive* | Liberty, equality and happiness for each individual; freedom for democratic nations | Cultural autonomy for each nation; a secure sense of belonging for individuals |
| Aspects which are generally regarded as *negative* | Expansion and imperialism in the name of liberty; the rise of expansive German nationalism | Forced conformity; racist tendencies; impending demands for "Lebensraum" |

**Figure 1: The pros and cons of nationalism**

group. Individuals are primarily particles in a social system, and their happiness cannot be promoted independently of the system that they belong to. The difference between the "English" and "German" attitudes towards freedom and security parallels in an obvious way the distinction between the negative "liberal" concept of liberty and the positive "continental" concept of liberty.[10]

The undesirable consequences of the two types of nationalism mostly flow from clashes between them. English liberalism, in its urge to further the liberty of individuals beyond national boundaries, inevitably tends to violate the national integrity and autonomy of traditionally-oriented nations. The German-type nationalists of those nations may respond to the intervention by demands for cultural self-determination. These demands are often upheld by appeals to the uniqueness and unity of the national culture, or *Volksgeist*, and the unity of opinion is frequently enforced by strongly conformist domestic policies. In the liberal camp, the conformist policies are seen as additional violations against individual rights, and it is possible that international pressure is applied to the traditionalist nation. As a consequence of the pressure, however, attitudes in the accused nation may become even more rigid, and myths about the purity of the race and *Lebensraum* may begin to gain popularity. At this point, it is usually difficult to see how the conflict might be solved peacefully.

## The unification of Europe

As we noted at the outset of this paper, the existence of the two types of European nationalism runs counter to the prevailing tendency towards economic unification in Europe. The representatives of the leading European countries all employ liberal, English-type arguments in their attempts to justify political and economic cooperation in Europe. The British demands for a free European market can be theoretically backed up with Lockean ideals regarding individual liberty. The French proposals concerning centralized political decision-making within the European Community are introduced in the name of democracy and wider participation. And the German emphasis on a harmonized and stable monetary policy can be supported by appeals to efficiency, security and general material welfare.

But there are two sets of problems which ought to be settled before these liberal arguments can be employed to justify European economic and political unification. Firstly, the liberal slogans are often mere disguises for the promotion of the national self-interest of the leading powers. Secondly, even the purest liberal policies carry with them the seeds of imperialism. Whenever either economic or political power has historically become centralized in any part of the world, the result has been the rise of German-type nationalism in the peripheral areas.

It is easy to discover at least some self-interested motives on the part of the

41

leading nations. English politicians, in their attempts to free the European market, are of course trying to create new opportunities to expand British industry. French decision-makers, in their turn, opt for the centralized political system in the hope that they can rule the Continent by taking over the bureaucratic machinery. And the Germans stress the importance of a stable monetary policy, since their own alleged expertise in that field would make them, by this criterion, the natural leaders of unified Europe. All these aspirations are an acceptable and understandable part of political life. But if these primary motives are hidden behind liberal and democratic slogans, it is fatally easy to ignore the equally legitimate political claims of smaller nations.

There are at least three ways in which the interests of smaller nations and peripheral areas may suffer from the impacts of economic and political unification in Europe. First, there are nations which cannot compete economically with multinational corporations. These nations may become the European colonies of the twenty-first century. Second, when all the important political decisions are made in the centre, the interests of the periphery are frequently forgotten. In Britain, for instance, the Scottish and Welsh national movements are probably based on this imbalance of power. Third, the multilingual and multinational nature of Europe is an obstacle for any attempts towards cultural unification.[11] Unless the new leaders are willing to resort to violence, it would seem that Europe will remain culturally diverse even in the future. But if this is the case, then the possibility of German-type nationalist reactions also remains. And claims for cultural autonomy can, as we have seen, become the source of tension, conflict and even warfare between the "liberal" and "traditionalist" nations.

Our conclusion is that the existence of the two types of European nationalism ought to be taken seriously when decisions concerning the unification of Europe are made. In practice, this implies two *directives* which should take precedence over all the present official directives of the European Community. First, the interests and aspirations of each state, nation and region should be carefully examined before decisions on international cooperation are made. This examination should, obviously, be conducted by independent social and political scientists rather than bureaucratic researchers who have vested interests in the unification process. Second, the present and future interests of individuals and nations should take precedence over the short-term interests of politicians and business executives. This requirement, albeit undoubtedly difficult to fulfil within the present political system, is implied by both main forms of European nationalism. These ethical directives, if implemented, would probably remove some of the maleficent nationalist tensions which stand in the way of European unification. But since their implementation is unlikely, the correct conclusion to be drawn from our considerations may also be that international cooperation in Europe has already gone far enough.

# Bibliographical references

*Bertelsmann Universal Lexikon in Farbe* Vol. 2 (1976) Berlin: Bertelsmann Lexikon-Verlag.

*Der Grosse Brockhaus Kompaktausgabe* Vol. 15 (1983) Wiesbaden: F.A. Brockhaus, eighteenth edition.

*Dizionario garzanti della lingua italiana* (1978) Milan: Aldo Garzanti Editore, sixteenth edition.

Gardels, N. (1991) "Two concepts of nationalism: An interview with Isaiah Berlin" *The New York Review of Books* No. 19, November 21: 19-23.

Gardiner, P. (Ed.) (1969) *Theories of History*, New York: Free Press.

Häyry, H. (1991) *The Limits of Medical Paternalism*, London and New York: Routledge.

Le Petit Robert: Dictionnaire alphabétique & analogique de la langue française (1973) Paris: Société du nouveau littré.

Locke, J. [1690] (1924) *Two Treatises of Government*, London: J.M. Dent & Sons Ltd.

Paine, T. [1776] (1986) *Common Sense*, Harmondsworth, Middlesex: Penguin Books.

Paine, T. [1791-92] (1985) *Rights of Man*, Harmondsworth, Middlesex: Penguin Books.

Rousseau, J.-J. [1762] (1986) *The Social Contract and Discourses*, London: J.M. Dent & Sons Ltd.

*The New Encyclopaedia Britannica* Vol. 8 (1989a) Chicago: Encyclopaedia Britannica, Inc., fifteenth edition.

*The New Encyclopaedia Britannica* Vol. 27 (1989b) Chicago: Encyclopaedia Britannica, Inc., fifteenth edition.

*The Pocket Oxford Dictionary of Current English* (1984) Ed. R.E. Allen. Oxford: Clarendon Press, seventh edition.

*The Random House Dictionary of the English Language* (1968) New York: Random House.

*Webster's Ninth New Collegiate Dictionary* (1983) Springfield, Massachusetts: Merriam-Webster Inc.

## Notes

Our thanks are due to two anonymous referees of the *International Journal of Moral and Social Studies*, whose critical comments forced us to improve our arguments considerably. Our thanks are also due to Mark Shackleton, Lecturer in English, University of Helsinki, for revising the language of the paper.

1. A brief but sound description of the types and development of nationalism can be found in *The New Encyclopaedia Britannica* (1989b, 468-71). Interesting viewpoints on the issue are provided by Gardels, 1991.

2. 1. Exaltation du sentiment national; attachement passionné à la nation à laquelle on appartient, accompagné parfois de xenophobie et d'une volonté d'isolement. ... 2. Doctrine fondée sur ce sentiment, subordonnant toute la politique intérieure au développement de la puissance nationale et revendiquant le droit d'affirmer à l'extérieur cette puissance sans limitation de souveraineté. ... 3. Doctrine, mouvement politique qui revendique pour une nationalité le droit de former une nation. (*Le Petit Robert*, 1973, s.v. nationalisme.)

3. Dottrina politica fondata sul prinzipio di nazionalità. (*Dizionario Garzanti della* 1978, s.v. *nazionalismo.*)

4. "Prinzipio in base al quale ogni nazione ha diritto di costituirsi in uno Stato indipendente" (*Dizionario Garzanti della* 1978, s.v. *nazionalità*).

5. "*Nationalismus*, die übersteigerte, aggressive Form des *National-bewußtseins*, die sich ... in der Franz. Revolution herausbildete. Der N. hat zwar das nationalstaatl. Europa des 19. u. der 1. Hälfte des 20. Jh. aufgebaut; andererseits hat er jedoch zu einseitiger u. rücksichtsloser Verfechtung national-egoist. Interessen unter Mißachtung der Lebens-rechte u. Lebenskräfte anderer Völker geführt. Der N. beruht auf dem Denkfehler, daß die Pflege u. Hochschätzung des Eigenen mit einer Geringschätzung u. Bekämpfung des Fremden verbunden sein müsse." (*Bertelsmann Universal Lexikon* 1976, s.v. *Nationalismus*)

6. "*Nationalismus*, die Ideologie, die den Gedanken der Nation und des auf ihr gegründeten (National-)Staates militant nach innen und außen vertritt. Je nach historisch-kultureller, ethn., polit. und sozioökonom. Ausgangs-lage zeigt der N. ein vielgestaltiges Bild: Verabsolutierung nationaler ... Interessen und Wünsche, Geringschätzung fremder Völker und nationaler

Minderheiten, Verbindung von Nationalbewußtsein (oder Nationalgefühl) mit Elite- und Sendungsbewußtsein oder mit Rassismus. Diese Merkmale müssen nicht immer alle zugleich oder mit der gleichen Intensität auftreten. Der N. kann von einer Bevölkerungsschicht oder von einem ganzen Volk getragen werden. Nationalist. Kräften dient er zur gewaltsamen Integration (Assimilation, Gleichschaltung) nach innen und zur aggressiven Expansion nach aussen. Der N. eines Volkes kann den eines anderen herausfordern und so ein Konfliktpotential erzeugen." (*Der Grosse Brockhaus* 1983, s.v. *Nationalismus*.)

7. In the latter part of the eighteenth century, the greatest pamphleteer for these ideals was Thomas Paine. See, e.g., Paine, 1776 and 1791-92.

8. The first English translation is from 1800. Extracts of the work can be found, e.g., in Gardiner, 1969. Herder studied philosophy in Königsberg under Immanuel Kant, and his theory anticipated G.W.F. Hegel's work on the philosophy of history.

9. Another botanical analogy, presented by Isaiah Berlin, is designed to explain the aggressive reactions against liberal expansionism. A wounded *Volksgeist*, according to Berlin, is "like a bent twig, forced down so severely that when released, it lashes back with fury". (Gardels, 1991, p 19.)

10. The sense in which we use the concepts of negative and positive liberty is explained in Häyry, 1991, pp 30-1, 36-7, 49.

11. In this respect, the United States of Europe would presumably resemble the late Soviet Union more than the United States of America. The cultural unification of Europe would not, it is to be hoped, start with the extermination of the aboriginal inhabitants, as was the case in North America.

# 4 The place of secession in liberal democratic theory

*Harry Beran*

Almost everyone who has written on the moral justification of secession agrees that secession is justified under some circumstances. But there is disagreement whether, within liberal democratic theory, there is a presumption in favour of permitting secession if it is desired or a presumption in favour of maintaining the unity of the state or no presumption either way. The three positions can be stated more fully as follows.

(1) The pro-separatist presumption: secession should be permitted, unless the state can show that it would lead to harm so great that it overrides the presumption in favour of permitting secession. To hold this presumption is consistent with the belief that stable political boundaries are valuable and that deep political disagreements should often be resolved by means other than secession. For to hold it is to claim, not that secession is normally a desirable method of resolving political disagreements, but that it should, normally, be permitted if it is desired.

(2) The pro-unity presumption: secession should be permitted only where the separatists suffer harm so great in the existing state that the presumption in favour of maintaining the unity of the state is overridden.

(3) There is no presumption either way: each case must be judged on its merits.

This paper will try to show that, in liberal democratic theory, the pro-separatist presumption is the most plausible position. The issue arises in utilitarian and non-utilitarian discussions of the justification of secession. The two types of discussion will be treated in turn. The following points will be taken for granted.

(1) The discussion takes a liberal democratic framework for granted. The writers discussed in the first section of the paper combine this with a utilitarian viewpoint, those discussed in the second section do not.

(2) The separatists are in a majority in their territory and would be viable after secession either as an independent state or with another group they wish to join. It will be assumed that plausible criteria of viability can be formulated.

47

(3) The separatists may be but need not be a nation, in the sense of this term that permits a distinction between nations and states.

(4) In the contemporary world a number of levels of political decision-making are needed: local, national, continental and world-wide. The issue of secession can arise at each level.[1]

(5) A group can have the moral right to do something, for example to secede, though this action is not in its best interests.


## Utilitarian discussions of the justification of secession

The main utilitarian discussions of secession are those by J. S. Mill (1962), Henry Sidgwick (1919) and Lee C. Buchheit (1978). Though all are utilitarians, the first accepts the pro-separatist presumption, the second the pro-unity presumption, the third a compromise between these positions. Perhaps it should be said at the outset that a reading of these writers leaves it unclear what a consistently utilitarian position on the justification of secession is.

As noted, Mill accepts the pro-separatist presumption, at least as far as nations are concerned. In a well-known passage he claims (1962: 361) that

> (w)here the sentiment of nationality exists in any force, there is a *prima facie* case for uniting all the members of the nationality under the same government, and a government to themselves apart. This is merely saying that the question of government ought to be decided by the governed. One hardly knows what any division of mankind should be free to do if not to determine with which of the various collective bodies of human beings they choose to associate themselves.

The significance of this claim depends partly on what Mill means by a nation. He defines nation, not in cultural terms, but in terms of a sentiment of solidarity which the members of a nation have for each other but do not have for other people. Objective features such as community of language, religion or race are among the causes of the feelings of solidarity which make a group a nation, but do not in themselves make them a nation. Thus the Swiss, according to Mill, are a distinct nation although they do not share a common language and indeed consist of groups which speak languages also spoken by members of other nations (1962: 360). Because Mill defines nations in terms of sentiments of solidarity, almost all groups that seek secession would be nations, in Mill's sense, distinct from those from whom they wish to separate. For, usually, the desire for secession is itself strong evidence that the separatists have little sense of solidarity with their fellow citizens.[2]

Clearly, Mill accepts, in the passage quoted above, a pro-separatist presumption regarding nations that wish to secede from multinational states.

He makes it equally clear that the same presumption holds if a fragment of a nation wishes to secede from a multinational state in order to join their fellow nationals in another state. He gives the example of an Italian province under French or German rule that wishes to join the other Italian provinces. He writes that in such a case "there is not only an obvious propriety, but, if either freedom or concord is cared for, a necessity, for breaking the connection" between the Italian province and the French or German state (1962: 366).

The only restriction on the exercise of the *prima facie* case for secession which Mill mentions is geographical. Such separation is impossible, he claims, if the two nations are intermingled in the same territory or if part of a nation is geographically separated from its fellow nationals by territory occupied by people of another nation and this part is "too weak to maintain separate independence" (1962: 363). It seems likely that Mill would have accepted that there can be other conditions that may override the *prima facie* case for independence where it is desired by a nation.

Mill appears to have three arguments for the pro-separatist presumption. Two have already been quoted. One is the argument from freedom: if one values freedom then one must accept a presumption in favour of divisions of mankind being free to choose with which other division they wish to be associated. The second argument already quoted is the argument from self-government: the question of government ought to be decided by the governed. This claim is most significant. For, in the context in which it is made, it appears to assert not just the commonplace that a given collectivity of citizens ought to be free to choose their government, but that part of a given collection of citizens, if they are a separate nation, ought to be free to secede. Mill's third argument for the claim that, *prima facie*, nations ought to be free to secede is that from the difficulty of maintaining free institutions in a multinational state. It is important to remember here that, according to Mill's definition of a nation, a multinational state is, by definition, a state composed of a number of groups of people who have no or very little feeling of solidarity for each other. According to Mill (1962: 362), free political institutions are next to impossible in a multinational state, for two reasons. First, if there is no fellow-feeling among people, then a united public opinion, which is necessary for the working of representative political institutions, cannot exist. This is so especially if the members of the multinational state speak different languages.[3] Second, if there is no fellow-feeling among the people, then the final barrier against government despotism is missing, viz. an army which has more sympathy for the people than for the government. For each nation in the multinational state can then be controlled by a part of the army drawn from other member nations of the state. He cites as an example the Austrian Empire which, he writes, ruled its Italian provinces with the help of the Hungarian regiments and its Hungarian provinces with the help of its Italian regiments (1962: 362).

Though asserting very clearly that *prima facie* each nation ought to have a distinct government of its own, Mill also points to the value of multinational federation. He claims that federation reduces the risk of war amongst the member nations and increases their protection against aggression from powerful states (1962: 366).

Mill makes some remarks which may appear to be inconsistent with his claim that *prima facie* each nation ought to have a distinct government of its own. The notorious passage runs as follows.

> Experience proves that it is possible for one nationality to ... be absorbed in another: and when it was originally an inferior and more backward portion of the human race the absorption is greatly to its advantage. Nobody can suppose that it is not more beneficial for a Breton, or a Basque of French Navarre, to be brought into the current of ideas and feelings of a highly civilised ... people - to be a member of the French nationality, admitted on equal terms to the privileges of French citizenship, sharing the advantages of French protection, and the dignity of French prestige and power - than to sulk on its own rocks, the half-savage relic of past times, revolving in his own little mental orbit, without participation or interest in the general movement of the world. The same remark applies to the Welshman or the Scottish Highlander as members of the British nation.

This passage can be interpreted so as to be consistent with Mill's claim that, *prima facie*, each nation should have a state of its own and should be free to choose which other groups politically to associate with. The passage asserts that it is beneficial for small, backward nations to be absorbed by larger and more advanced ones. But Mill can be said also to believe, though he does not explicitly say so, that small, backward nations, nevertheless, are free to have political independence should they desire it; and that this is so even if they are already part of a multinational state. In short, he can be interpreted to believe that if the Breton were (in Mill's day) still a distinct nation then they were free to establish a state of their own, but that they would be better off if they permitted themselves to be absorbed into the French nation. This position merely relies on the plausible claim that one can be free to do something which is not the best thing for one. Admittedly the distinction involved is not one that can be made by every version of utilitarianism, but that is another issue.

Sidgwick (1919) accepts the pro-unity presumption. He agrees with Mill on a number of points. Like Mill, he distinguishes between state and nation. Like Mill, he defines the nation, not in terms of cultural distinctness, but in terms of a "sentiment of unity or fellow-citizenship" (1919: 224). Like Mill, he gives the Swiss as an example of a group who, he claims, are one nation, despite differences of language and religion, because they share a "community of patriotic sentiment" (1919: 224). But this is as far as his agreement with Mill

50

goes. He notes that in the Europe of his day it is held desirable that a state be co-extensive with a single nation, but asserts that the interests of separatists are never sufficient for a right of secession or, as he also calls it, a right of disruption (1919: 226). According to Sidgwick (1919: 226), such a right exists only if the separatists suffer one or more of the following grievances: (1) severe oppression, (2) gross misgovernment or (3) persistent and harsh opposition to their legitimate desires. In short, Sidgwick believes there is a presumption in favour of the unity of existing states and that a group that wishes to disrupt this unity has a right to do so only if it suffers great harm from the existing government.

Sidgwick (1919: 226-9) gives the following six arguments in support of his claim that there is no right of secession simply in virtue of distinct nationhood or because it is in the interests of the separatists. (1) Secession reduces the power and prestige of the existing state by making it smaller and it reduces its power by increasing the number of its potential foes. (2) If secession occurred there would be a minority in the new state who are against secession and who would suffer whether they remained in the new state or moved to the rump of the old state. (3) Secession may deprive the existing state of natural resources it does not have in the rump of its territory. (4) If the separatists do not accept a fair share of the national debt, secession would result in an increase of this debt per person in the rump state; if they do accept a share of the debt, it would be difficult to enforce the agreement. (5) Secession may destroy the natural boundaries of a state. This is undesirable since such boundaries promote peace, for they help in defence but not in attack. (6) It must be taken into account that the community from which secession is proposed will dislike the loss of territory involved. This territorial sentiment must be recognised as an important force operating in favour of existing borders.

Towards the end of The Elements of Politics, Sidgwick (1919: 649-50) returns to the topic of secession and adds a seventh argument against a general right of secession. Perhaps the argument is intended to be a *reductio*. He claims that if a general right of secession were accepted, there would be no reason why it should be restricted to territorially concentrated groups. This is so, he argues, because the inconvenience caused by secession is no greater if the separatists are not territorially concentrated, in other words if secession results in two independent states with intermingled citizens operating in the same territory.

In addition to the conditions already listed, which Sidgwick specifies as creating a right of secession, he also mentions further conditions under which it should be permitted, if it is desired (1919: 649). These conditions, which point to an inappropriate political unity of two populations, are: (1) the two portions of a state's territory are separated by a long interval of sea, or other physical obstacles, from any very active intercommunication; (2) the two populations of a state have divergent needs and demand very different things from their government because of differences of race, religion, history or social

51

conditions; (3) the external relations of the two populations of a state would be quite different, if they had independent states, from what they are under one government; as a result each population may lose more through risk of involvement in the other population's quarrels than it gains from the military power of the existing state.

Sidgwick does not present this supplementary case for secession very clearly. One possible interpretation of his remarks is that in each of the three cases the true interests of both populations are promoted by disrupting the existing state and, therefore, if one of the two populations wished to secede, secession should be permitted. However, since the three conditions mentioned do not necessarily involve oppression, misgovernment or harsh opposition to legitimate desires of the separatists, they do not create a right of secession.

One further part of Sidgwick's book is relevant to secession, that which deals with conquest. Some writers claim (see Birch below) that a group has the right of secession if they have been incorporated into a state by conquest. Sidgwick does not include past conquest in his list of conditions that create the right of secession. But he notes (1919: 311) that the conquest of one state by another of roughly equal civilisation is, "under ordinary circumstances, rightly disapproved by the morality of modern civilised nations". The reasons he gives for concurring with this disapproval are, first, that the conquest results in a state with parts not united by national sentiment, a state of affairs likely to last for an indefinite period, and, second, that government of the conquered by the conquerors is unlikely to confer benefits which outweigh the drawback of alien rule.

In summary, Sidgwick believes that there is a presumption to maintain the unity of the state in the face of a demand for secession and that the right of secession exists only where the separatists are suffering great harm in the existing state. But Sidgwick also appears to hold that there can be cases where, although there is no right of secession, it is desirable that secession be permitted, if it is desired. The two cases that seem to fall into this category are where the parts of a state form an inappropriate unity (of which Sidgwick gives three examples) and where one state has conquered another of equal civilisation.

Buchheit is the third utilitarian who has discussed the moral justification of secession. In his book Secession (1978) he aims to offer a rational normative scheme for the determination of secessionist legitimacy (1978: 217-18, 237). He sketches positions on the legitimacy of secession similar to those of Mill (the pro-separatist presumption) and Sidgwick (the pro-unity presumption), but accepts the third of the positions on secession noted at the beginning of this paper: morally, each case of desired secession must be judged on its merits (1978: 224-5, 227, 238-9). He claims this should be done from a utilitarian viewpoint — but perhaps with a conservative state-centred bias (1978: 227). He rejects the pro-unity presumption (the remedial model as he calls it) because, he claims, this position "cannot accommodate the plea of an unquestionably valid 'self', which is not oppressed, but which is capable of separating from its present state with very little disruption to itself, its governors, or the international community" (1978: 238). He rejects the pro-separatist presumption (the parochialist model, as he calls it) because, he claims, it ignores the economic, political and strategic cost of secession (1978: 224, 238).

According to Buchheit (1978: 228), a morally legitimate claim to secessionist self-determination must: (1) involve a "self", (2) involve, moreover, a self capable of independent existence or willing to become part of an existing viable political entity, (3) be likely to result in greater world harmony (or less global disruption) than maintaining the unity of the existing state. The self in the first condition is a culturally distinct community with its own territory. Viability, in the second condition, is to be understood in economic and political terms. In the third condition, the effect of secession on world harmony is judged by comparing the disruption caused by maintaining the unity of the existing state to the disruption that would be caused by permitting secession. The three conditions are not necessary conditions for the moral legitimacy of secession. The more one condition is satisfied the less the others need be. The moral legitimacy of secession is calculated by weighing the extent to which the three conditions are satisfied. If the separatists are a full-blooded self, would be viable after secession and secession would improve world harmony, then secession is unquestioningly morally legitimate. Obviously, a group that has little claim to distinct selfhood, a low viability rating after secession and whose secession would reduce world harmony, has no case for secession. Equally obviously, the difficult cases are those where there are conflicting indications. Buchheit uses the example of East Pakistan to explain how he intends the conditions of legitimate secession to operate, especially in hard-to-decide cases. He regards East Pakistan, just before its secession from West Pakistan, as a distinct self but as economically unviable, i.e. economically dependent on international aid. Hence the first condition is satisfied, the second not. But Buchheit believes that East Pakistan was suffering great oppression from West Pakistan and that without secession there would have been a high risk of civil war between the two parts of Pakistan or of war between Pakistan and India. Therefore, the third condition for legitimate secession is met to a very high degree and East Pakistan scores fairly highly on the three conditions of legitimate secession combined. Buchheit adds that East Pakistan would have scored too poorly to justify secession, if it had not been a distinct self or, while being a distinct self, had not suffered oppression.

What can be learnt from these three utilitarian discussions of the justification of secession? Sidgwick's discussion of secession reads like a response to Mill's and Buchheit's like a response to Mill's and Sidgwick's. Mill accepts the pro-separatist presumption; Sidgwick, noting the pro-separatist presumption, accepts the opposite, pro-unity presumption; and Buchheit, noting both presumptions, rejects both and claims that each case has to be judged on its merits. But neither Sidgwick nor Buchheit explicitly refers to their theoretical forerunner(s), nor do they address the precise arguments their forerunner(s) offer for their positions. And, most unfortunately, none of the three writers explicitly derives his position on the justification of secession from a clearly formulated utilitarian starting point. Mill and Sidgwick are, of course, hedonistic utilitarians of a sort. Buchheit does not indicate what version of utilitarianism his "utilitarian viewpoint" is. Since the three writers differ so much in their views on the moral justification of secession, their discussions of it leave it unclear what a consistently utilitarian position on secession is.

It is not very useful for someone who does not accept utilitarianism to attempt to formulate a utilitarian position on the justification of secession. But it may be helpful to raise three issues that a utilitarian position has to deal with. To do this economically a specific version of utilitarianism has to be used. Following Kymlicka's (1990: Ch. 2) critical discussion of utilitarianism, I will use a restricted, rational preference version of it in which the preferences of different persons are given equal weight. To say the version is restricted means that the utilitarian principle is applied not to issues of personal choice of action, but only to issues of public policy. And what is maximised is neither happiness nor any other mental state, nor the satisfaction of people's actual preferences, but the satisfaction of their rational preferences, i.e. preferences based on adequate information and correct judgements.

It is a contentious issue among rational preference utilitarians whether all rational preferences should count in the attempt to maximise utility or whether some should not. Should a sadist's preference to inflict pain on others count as much as the others' preference not to have pain inflicted on them? A similar question can be asked about preferences regarding secession. Typically, separatists are a minority of the existing state, even if they are a majority in the separatist region. Therefore, if, in determining public policy regarding the permissibility of secession, the preferences of all members of the state count, the policy would be against secession. This would be in the spirit of Sidgwick's position. For his sixth objection to a general right of secession is that the community from which secession is proposed would dislike the loss of territory. But, if only the preferences of the people in the separatist region count in determining public policy regarding the permissibility of secession, then, if most people in this region want secession, it would usually be permissible. This would be in the spirit of Mill's position, according to which people should be free to decide with which other groups they are politically associated.[4] Two questions arise. First, can utilitarians give good reasons for determining whether all preferences should count or only those of the people in the separatist region? Second, if the preferences of all citizens count, is this compatible with the principle of freedom of association, a central principle of liberalism? The issue is, of course, a quite general one regarding membership in groups. If the

54

preferences of all members of the state have to be counted to determine whether secession by a minority is morally permissible, must the preferences of all members of a family be counted to determine whether divorce is morally permissible?

So far only the preferences of members of the state with a separatist group have been mentioned. But Buchheit proposes that the justification of secession be assessed in terms not just of the state concerned but in terms of its effect on world harmony. Translating Buchheit's view into preference utilitarianism, this raises the question whose preferences should be taken into account in assessing the justification of a particular case of secession: those of the people living in the separatist region, those of the members of the state with a separatist movement or those of everyone in the world. If the last alternative is the one required by utilitarianism, then this would seem to allow for the possibility that the preference of most members of a given state to permit secession from it could be outweighed by the preferences of most members of other states to preserve the status quo.

A second issue for a utilitarian theory of secession can be posed by comparing Buchheit's and Sidgwick's approach to assessing the morality of secession. According to Sidgwick a group has the right of secession if it suffers severe oppression or gross misgovernment or great opposition to its legitimate desires. Buchheit offers three rather different conditions for the moral legitimacy of secession: the separatists have to be a self, moreover a self that would be viable after secession, and secession has to lead to greater world harmony (or less global disruption) than maintaining the unity of the state. If the separatists fail either the first two conditions or the third condition completely, secession is not justified, e.g. if the separatists are a genuine self that would be viable after secession, but secession would result in a great increase in global disruption. Buchheit's approach shows that Sidgwick's account of the morality of secession cannot be a complete account. A group may have the right of secession, but the group would be wrong to exercise the right if doing so would cause a world war that would make the separatists and millions of other people worse off. However, Buchheit's account of the matter is also unsatisfactory because it glosses over the important distinction between the following two questions.

(1) Morally speaking, should a given group of separatists be permitted to secede? This question must be answered without taking into account whether any other groups are likely to prevent secession by force. It has to be answered in terms of such considerations as to whether the unity of the state should be voluntary or whether certain kinds of harm suffered by separatists, such as those listed by Sidgwick, justify disrupting the state. Only after this question is answered, can the further question, whether attempted secession may justifiably be prevented by force, be answered.

(2) Given that the separatists ought to be permitted to secede, should they attempt to secede? To this question the likelihood that force, even if

illegitimate, will be used in an attempt to prevent secession, is relevant. Even if justice is completely on the side of the separatists, their attempt to secede may be morally wrong if it would be likely to result in global war.

Three of the six arguments of Sidgwick's, already listed above, for the claim that there is no general right of secession, point to a third issue that utilitarian (and other) theories of secession have to deal with; they point to the need for ideal world theory as well as non-ideal world theory of secession. These arguments are his third: secession may deprive the existing state of natural resources it does not have in the rest of its territory; his fourth: the separatists may not pay a fair share of the national debt of the existing state; and his fifth: secession may alter the boundaries of the existing state in such a way as to leave it more vulnerable in war. These arguments would lose their force in a world in which the benefits of exploiting natural resources are shared justly among states, in which international agreements are kept and in which warfare has been abandoned. No doubt utilitarians would accept that such a world is better than one which lacks these features. Therefore, utilitarians, and others, should develop two kinds of theory of secession: first a theory for a world in which international morality is complied with, and only then a theory for a world in which it is only partially complied with.[5]

## Non-utilitarian discussions of the justifiability of secession.[6]

In previous papers (1984, 1988a) I have argued for the pro-separatist presumption. According to the version of liberal democratic theory I accept, biologically normal adults have the moral right of personal self-determination and, therefore, the moral right to determine their political relationships. Therefore, individual members of the state must be free to emigrate and groups which have a communal right to the territory they occupy must be free to secede.[7] The right of emigration is not sufficient to make political relationships voluntary, since large groups usually cannot find anywhere to move to, especially as intact communities. At any rate it is plausible that a community that is the traditional occupant of a territory has a moral right to continue to inhabit this territory.[8] Therefore, if the members of this community wish to exercise their right of personal self-determination by removing themselves from their state, they must be allowed to do this with their territory, i.e. by seceding. In short, according to liberal democratic theory, those political divisions of humanity are, normally, rightful which reflect the willingness of people to live together in separate units.

To claim this is not to deny that there are substantive criteria for making choices about the size or unity of a state. It is to claim that the judgement whether it is in their interests to remain part of an existing state must be left to the separatists and that if they judge that they would be better off after secession, the rest of the state is not, normally, justified in enforcing the maintenance of the existing political relationship. But of course circumstances can make it impossible for the separatists to act on their desire for secession and weighty moral considerations can override the presumption in favour of permitting secession.

Kai Nielsen (1993) appears to accept the pro-separatist presumption, but it is unclear whether he intends it to apply only to groups that are nations, in the sense of culturally distinct entities, or also to other groups that are a majority in their homeland and respect the rights of others. Nielsen asserts that there is a moral right of secession, this being a right that can be exercised without the right-holding group having to show that it is the victim of injustice. He sees the right of secession as a unilateral right, a no-fault right, on the model of no-fault divorce (1993: 35). But Nielsen appears to veer between asserting a right of secession based on the need to preserve and promote a distinct national identity and asserting a right of secession based on the right of groups to determine their own affairs according to their wishes, whether they have a cultural identity distinct from their neighbours or not. The latter, more permissive, doctrine appears to be expressed in the claim that "we must ... accept the right of persons who are extensively predominant in a distinct territory to determine their common destiny provided they do not violate the civil liberties of others, including, of course, minorities who live in the same territory" (1993: 29). According to the less permissive doctrine only groups which have a cultural identity have this right (1993: 34). But even if it is the nationalist doctrine Nielsen intends to assert, it is not clear how much less permissive it is, since Nielsen not only asserts that Quebec meets the conditions for having the moral right of secession, but also asks (but does not answer) whether Prince Edward Island could form a feasible nation-state despite its small size (1993: 39). If a degree of cultural distinctness as small as that of Prince Edward Island from the other two Maritime Provinces (Nova Scotia and New Brunswick) or from the rest of Anglophone Canada is sufficient distinctness for the right of secession, then the cultural distinctness criterion places very low limits on candidates for this right. That Nielsen intends the cultural distinctness criterion to be applied very generously is also suggested by his remark that it is satisfied if people "*perceive* themselves as having a distinct culture and tradition" (1993: 30, stress added).[9]

Anthony H. Birch (1984: 598, 1989) and Allen Buchanan (1991: 109) explicitly assert that there is a presumption against secession, a presumption that can be overridden only by weighty considerations. Michla Pomerance (1982: 73-6) appears to believe that there is no presumption either way. Pomerance asserts that there is a moral right of self-determination (including a right to independence and, therefore, secession), but that this right must be balanced against other equally important rights and principles (e.g. the right of territorial integrity and the need to preserve international peace and security) and that, therefore, the approach to self-determination issues must be a flexible one, encompassing a plethora of possible solutions, and resulting, in particular cases, in that solution best suited to particular circumstances. Since Pomerance does not argue for the position he sketches, it will not be further discussed here. Instead Birch's and Buchanan's position, involving the pro-unity presumption, will be stated more fully and discussed.

According to Birch (1984, 1989: 63-66) a group has the right of secession if they are the majority in their region and if one or more of the following conditions hold: (1) their region has been incorporated into the state by force and they have never given full consent to the union; (2) the national government fails, in a serious way, to protect the basic rights and security of the region; (3) the democratic system has failed to safeguard the legitimate political and economic interests of the region; (4) the national government has rejected a bargain which was entered between the region and other parts of the state in order to preserve the essential interests of the region from being overridden by the national majority. Birch notes that further reflection may lead to the inclusion of other conditions that, with a majority vote for secession, would be sufficient to create a right of secession.[10]

Buchanan's (1991: 29-70) conditions for a right of secession are broadly similar to, though not identical with, Birch's. But, most importantly, the two writers agree that there is a presumption in favour of maintaining the unity of the state, a presumption which can be overridden only by a small number of weighty moral reasons. Clearly their position is very similar to that of Sidgwick, though each writer offers a somewhat different list of the small number of moral reasons that override the pro-unity presumption. But they differ from Sidgwick in not relying on utilitarianism as a moral foundation for their views. Buchanan notes that he prefers not to derive his normative theory of secession from any foundational ethical theory, but from the "most widely held and least controversial moral views" (1991: xiii). Birch does not mention what basic moral principles he relies on in his normative theory of secession, but could be understood to be using only generally accepted moral principles. Both writers explicitly formulate their theories within a liberal framework.

Birch and Buchanan give a number of arguments for the pro-unity presumption. Birch, in *Nationalism and National Integration*, (1989: 64) claims that "(l)iberal systems of government could not be sustained if any minority with a temporary grievance used this as a reason for opting out of the system", but, in this book, gives no support for this claim. However, on a previous occasion (1984) he offered four arguments for the pro-unity presumption. None is persuasive.[11]

First, he claims that liberal democracy provides a fair procedure for reaching collective decisions about government policy. Since groups have the right of voice in liberal democracies and, therefore, the opportunity to influence policy, they do not need the right of exit as well (1984: 598). Reply: if liberty is a fundamental value of a society, the society must grant not only the right of voice but also that of exit; not only the procedures but also the unity of the state must be voluntarily accepted. No doubt Birch would not wish to claim that individual citizens do not need the right of emigration because they have the right of political participation. So why should the right of participation make unnecessary the right of secession?

Second, Birch claims that "if groups have assented to the system in the first place it is unreasonable that they should walk out, with all the disruption this would cause, just because some decisions or elections go against them" (1984: 598). Reply: let it be assumed that a group has indeed assented not only to "the system", but also to being part of the state which has the system. Perhaps they had the choice between being independent or joining a federation and chose the latter course in a referendum. Let it also be assumed that we are talking about the people that voted in the referendum, not their descendants. Although these assumptions hold for very few groups in the world, they make it possible to focus clearly on the main issue Birch raises in his present argument, i.e. whether, within (democratic) liberalism, a group's assent to be part of a system is revocable or irrevocable. Birch appears to lean towards the latter view. For he asserts that, if a group has assented to being part of a state, it can be justified in seceding only if it suffers from one or more of certain substantial grievances against the central government or the political system. I on the other hand follow Frederic Schick (1980) in asserting that, within liberalism, contracts should not be irrevocable. The claim is the normative one that consistent liberals should not demand that people enter lifelong irrevocable contracts. It should be possible to terminate contractual relationships, if appropriate with fair compensation being paid by the party that wishes prematurely to terminate the contract to the party that wishes to maintain it. The case for the claim that contracts should not be irrevocable is particularly strong in the political realm, which involves indefinite time periods and unforeseeable changes.

If a group wishes to secede it is bound to have reasons for wishing to do so. According to Birch these reasons must be weighty enough to override the pro-unity presumption. But if liberty is a fundamental political value, what is primary, in determining whether a group should be permitted to secede, is the loss of willingness of a group to maintain the unity of the state, not the adequacy of the reasons they have for wishing to secede. An argument from domestic analogy supports this view. Secession is like divorce. In the last few decades, in liberal democracies, there has been a shift of social policy regarding divorce from one where divorce was granted only if there were specified grounds which were deemed to justify divorce (adultery, cruelty, etc.) to a policy of permitting divorce if the relationship has broken down. This can be demonstrated by mutual consent to divorce or, if only one partner wishes to end the relationship, by that partner living apart from the other for a specified period. Similarly, secession should be permitted if a group shows clearly that it is no longer willing to be part of the existing state and without having to demonstrate that there are publicly recognised grievances which justify secession.[12]

The discussion of Birch's second argument for the pro-unity presumption shows that proponents of the pro-unity and pro-separatist presumptions take different normative approaches to the issue of secession. Proponents of the pro-unity presumption require that separatists have moral reasons for secession which justify disrupting the existing state. But proponents of the pro-separatist presumption reject this. They claim that if a group no longer wishes to be part of a state they ought to be permitted to leave whether they have an adequate substantive case for leaving or not. Indeed they may not have an adequate case; it may be in their interests not to secede, but within liberal democratic principles this does not justify the majority in not letting them go. Hence to discuss the issue of secession within liberal democratic theory as one of the justification, rather than the permissibility, of secession already begs the question against the pro-separatist presumption, against the conception of the liberal democratic state as a voluntary association.

Third, Birch claims that a right of secession would create instability within states if groups "could threaten to withdraw any time they disliked the decision favoured by the majority" (1984: 598-9). Reply: Birch exaggerates; if a group threatens to secede every time it loses a vote, its threat will become ineffective. Nevertheless, it is, of course, true that minorities have greater bargaining power in a state where their right of secession is recognised. But it is not clear that liberal democrats should reject this. Such a right may enable minorities to extract unfair concessions from majorities that do not wish them to secede. But it would also give minorities an effective response to the tyranny of the majority.

Fourth, Birch claims a right of secession of territorially concentrated groups would be unfair to minorities not so concentrated since they could not use the threat of secession as a bargaining point. Reply: this is analogous to arguing that a territorially concentrated minority in a federal state should not be permitted to adopt provincial status because another equally numerous minority is not territorially concentrated and therefore cannot have such a status. Facts can rightly make a difference as to whether a certain right exists or at least as to whether the right can be exercised. A human being literally incapable of benefiting from education has no right to education or at least is incapable of exercising the right. Similarly a territorially concentrated group may have a right of secession whereas a similar group not so concentrated may not.

I turn to Buchanan's case for the pro-unity presumption. He grants that, because of the value liberalism places on liberty, there would seem to be a presumption in favour of permitting secession if a group wants it and does not, by seceding, harm others (1991: 29-32). But he asserts that this presumption does not hold if the territory of the separatists is part of the legitimate territory of the existing state. For secession would then be the wrongful taking of part of the state's legitimate territory (1991: 109). So what makes something the legitimate territory of a state? According to Buchanan, the relationship between the state and its territory is that between an agent (the state) and a principal (the citizens of the state) who authorises the state to act on its behalf (1991: 108). A region is part of the legitimate territory of a state if "the people" (1991: 108-109) have authorised a state to perform certain functions within this territory.

The relationship between people, state and territory which Buchanan sketches is plausible within liberal democratic theory. But it is one that seems to make it particularly difficult to explain why secession must be the wrongful taking of territory. If the people are the principal in the political unit and the state merely its agent, then the primary right to the territory of the state must belong to the people, not the state. But then, why cannot part of the people sack the agent and appoint a new one, independent from the previous agent, in its part of the territory? Buchanan does not consider this question. What could be said to show that this would have to be the wrongful taking of territory? It could be claimed that the whole of the existing territory of the state belongs collectively to the whole of the existing people of the state. But how could the relationship between the citizens and the territory of a state be essentially collective within an individualist liberal theory of the relationship between people, territory and state? It seems at least as plausible to claim that, within such a theory, if a group rightfully occupies part of the territory of the existing state, that territory primarily belongs to that group.

Buchanan stresses that the state acts as an agent for a principal which includes not just the present generation of citizens but also future generations of citizens, that it safeguards the territory not just for the present generation but also for future ones. He stresses this point so much in his discussion of the objection to secession from the wrongful taking of territory (1991: 104-114, esp. 106-109) that one must assume he thinks it makes a difference to the justification of secession. But he does not explain why it does, nor is it clear why it should. If the relationship among the living citizens of the state, the state and their territory is such that secession would not, normally, be the wrongful taking of territory, it is unclear how reference to the future descendants of the present citizens could make it wrongful.

Buchanan offers two further considerations which he claims have to be balanced against the presumption in favour of secession possibly created by the value placed on liberty by liberalism. The first consideration is the value of majority rule. Buchanan claims (1991: 133) that even if the legitimacy of secession is accepted in principle, it must be balanced against the value of majority rule. This can be achieved, he suggests, by requiring more than a simple majority in favour of secession before it is permitted or by imposing a secession tax on the secessionists. Reply: this argument begs a very important question about the use that can be made of the majority principle in relation

61

to separatism. Clearly, if a group of liberal democrats want to be members of one state, they must also agree to settle some issues by majority vote. But it is not at all clear whether a separatist issue is properly settled by majority vote among all citizens of the existing state. For if such a vote were morally binding on the separatists then their membership of the state would no longer be voluntary. But if freedom is a fundamental value of democratic liberalism, the unity of the state should be based on the willingness of all regional groups within it to be part of it.

The second consideration which Buchanan claims must be balanced against any possible presumption in favour of permitting secession is the interest of people "in avoiding fragmentation that may increase dangers to national security by reducing the scale of the political unit below that required for adequate self-defence" (1991: 133). Reply: let it be ignored that the argument is anachronistic; in the nuclear age, no state has adequate self-defence. Even against conventional weapons, few states have adequate self-defence without alliances and a state newly reduced in size by secession is as free to enter such an alliance as any other state. But a much more important question is why Buchanan believes that the majority in a liberal democratic community has the right to force a political relationship on an unwilling minority for the sake of its military power. Finally, this objection to a general right of secession, as already noted in response to Sidgwick's fifth argument against a general right of secession, applies only in a world or region where war is likely to occur.

Perhaps a consistently worked out utilitarian position on secession would agree with something like Sidgwick's pro-unity presumption. But this raises the question whether utilitarianism is compatible with a version of democratic liberalism to which the voluntary nature of human relationships is central. Birch and Buchanan, who make liberal democratic theory combined with generally accepted moral principles their starting point for a normative theory of secession, agree with Sidgwick's pro-unity presumption and, like Sidgwick, offer a small number of weighty moral reasons which override this presumption and justify secession. I have tried to show that their arguments against the pro-separatist presumption are weak.

# Bibliography

Barry, Brian; 1983, "Self-Government Revisited" in D. Miller and L. Siedentop (eds) *The Nature of Political Theory*, Oxford: Clarendon Press, 1983.

Beran, Harry; 1984, "A liberal theory of secession", *Political Studies*, Vol. XXXII, pp. 21-31.

Beran, Harry; 1988a, "More theory of secession: a response to Birch", *Political Studies*, Vol. XXXVI, pp. 316-23.

Beran, Harry; 1988b, "Self-Determination: a Philosophical Perspective", in Macartney (1988).

Beran, Harry; 1993, "Border disputes and the right of national self-determination", *History of European Ideas*, Vol. 16, pp. 479-86.

Birch, Anthony H.; 1984, "Another liberal theory of secession", *Political Studies*, Vol. XXXII, pp. 596-602.

Birch, Anthony H.; 1989, *Nationalism and National Integration*, London and Boston: Unwin Hyman.

Brilmayer, Lea; 1991, "Secession and Self-Determination: A Territorial Interpretation", *The Yale Journal of International Law*, Vol. 16, pp. 177-201.

Buchanan, Allen; 1991, *Secession*, Boulder: Westview Press.

Buchheit, Lee C.; 1978, *Secession*, New Haven, Conn.: Yale University Press.

Kymlicka, Will; 1990, *Contemporary Political Philosophy*, Oxford: Clarendon Press.

Macartney, W.J. Allan; 1988, *Self-Determination in the Commonwealth*, Aberdeen: Aberdeen University Press.

MacCormick, Neil; 1988, "Self-Determination and the Determinacy of Selves" in Macartney (1988).

Mill, J. S.; 1962, (1859-1861) Utilitarianism, Liberty, Representative Government, London: Dent.

Nielsen, Kai; 1992, "Rights and Consequences: It All Depends", *Canadian*

*Journal of Legal Studies*, Vol. 7, pp. 63-94.

Nielsen, Kai; 1993, "Secession: The Case of Quebec", *Journal of Applied Philosophy*, Vol. 10, pp. 29-43.

Pogge, Thomas, W.; 1992, "Cosmopolitanism and Sovereignty", *Ethics*, Vol. 103, pp. 48-75.

Pomerance, Michla; 1982, *Self-Determination in Law and Practice*, the Hague: Nijhoff.

Schick, Frederic; 1980, "Towards a logic of liberalism", *Journal of Philosophy*, Vol. LXXVII, pp. 80-98.

Sidgwick, Henry; 1919, (1891) *The Elements of Politics*, 4th edn, London: Macmillan.

Walzer, Michael; 1983, *Spheres of Justice*, Oxford: Blackwell.

## Notes

1.  See Beran (1988b) and Pogge (1992).
2.  The difficulties of defining nationality in terms of sentiments of solidarity are explored in Beran (1993).
3.  Given Mill's definition of the nation in terms of sentiments of solidarity, it is of course quite possible for a state to contain a number of nations that all speak one language. On Mill's conception of the nation, the Croats, Serbs and Bosnians of former Yugoslavia, all speakers of Serbo-Croat, are separate nations because they do not share sufficient sentiments of solidarity.
4.  Brian Barry (1983) adopts a position on political boundaries very reminiscent of Mill's, but without reference to the latter. Like Mill, he defines nationality in terms of a group's common sentiment of solidarity (1983: 136-7) and claims that "there is a strong prima-facie case ... for drawing state boundaries so that they correspond with nationality ... as ... defined ..." (1983: 143). Barry mentions Sidgwick's objection to this from the dislike citizens have of losing part of their territory but takes it for granted that not all desires are morally relevant and, in particular, regards "the desire to hold territory for no reason other than that one has a strong desire to do so as morally irrelevant" (1983: 143).
5.  I am here indebted to Neil MacCormick (1988: 113) who claims that "... only reflection at the level of ideal theory followed by careful and rigorous

adjustment to the realities of the actual situation makes possible a principled approach in politics".

6.    The following discussions of the justifiability of secession are non--utilitarian, not in the sense that all the writers involved are known not to be utilitarians, but in the sense that they do not rely on any version of utilitarianism in arguing for their positions.

7.    The right of personal self-determination of a group of people is not sufficient to give them the right of secession. They must also have the right to remove the territory they inhabit from the existing state, otherwise they have to satisfy their desire to leave their state by emigration, not secession (Brilmayer 1991). Perhaps a group that has made a communal life in a territory has the right not only to remove itself but also its territory from their state, but much more needs to be said on this issue then I can say now.

8.    The need of other people for a place to live may require that people with surplus territory permit immigration into their territory or, if they do not wish to accept migrants, that they give up part of their territory by moving closer together (Walzer 1983: 46-8). However, more needs to be said about this: it is not clear that people who manage to prevent overpopulation may be driven from some of their land by people who fail to prevent it.

9.    Nielsen's doctrine has been mentioned among non-utilitarian treatments of secession, since the version of consequentialism he accepts "is a weak form" of it "which is distinguished from utilitarian consequentialism" (Nielsen 1992: 63).

10.   A writer's assertion of the moral right of secession does not commit the writer to the pro-separatist presumption. Sidgwick, Birch and Buchanan all assert the right of secession, but permit the excercise of the right only under relatively stringent conditions and can, therefore, consistently assert the right of secession and the pro-unity presumption.

11.   The following rebuttal of Birch's case for the pro-unity presumption is a revised version of that previously presented in Beran (1988a).

12.   See Beran (1984: 23) and Nielsen (1993: 35).

# 5 The ethics of national self-determination

*David George*

What used to be called, and occasionally still is called, 'the national question' can be posed in several ways. "Can present state boundaries, which have been drawn by, and in the interest of past holders of power, be redrawn on rational criteria?", is one way. Another is to ask, "Is the nationalist criterion for redrawing frontiers, namely, the principle and/or right of national self-determination, morally desirable?" This essay attempts to answer 'the national question' when put in that second way. But before that can be done it is necessary to examine the concept of national self-determination whose moral desirability is in question, and the obvious place at which to begin is with its conceptualisation in international law.

## I

Self-determination is a right of all peoples in international law,[1] though what this right includes, and to whom it applies, are controversial legal issues. The common first article of the two International Covenants on Human Rights, adopted by the UN General Assembly in 1966, declares: "All peoples have the right of self-determination. By virtue of that right they freely determine their political status and freely pursue their economic, social and cultural development", though neither here nor in any other international legal document is the bearer and beneficiary of this right, the 'people', defined.[2] Several jurists have argued the ambiguity this creates is resolved by current state and UN practice which restricts the right to colonies; to trust, non self-governing and mandated territories; and to citizens subject to racist regimes, i.e. to groups which are generally accepted as political units and whose basis of association therefore includes a territorial element with stable boundaries.[3] Current practice is not criterionless then, but to confine self-determination to this type of group implies an arbitrary stipulation of the meaning of 'peoples' and hence an unduly restrictive application of the right. Human groups lacking a territorial basis and concomitant degree of institutional organisation are ineligible for self-determination, a formula which would appear to exclude national minorities within a state such as the Bretons, the Basques or the Scots. Since that is its effect it is unsuitable for present purposes as these are precisely the kind of groups which are normally thought of as bearers of a moral right of self-determination. In what follows I will assume group self-determination also applies to nations, understood either as involuntary ethnic or cultural communities or, alternatively, as voluntary associations based on shared sentiments and solidarity.[4]

The scope of the right of national self-determination is also doubtful in international law. Entitlements do include a right of secession to form a new state or to join an existing state if it is willing, as well a right to attain a measure of political autonomy short of independent statehood (e.g. the Cook Islands association with New Zealand), or simply to choose to remain within an existing state. This is what is meant by a people determining its political status. Whether this includes choosing a non-state form of political organisation is legally dubious, though logically implied. What is to count as external interference in respect of a people freely determining its political status is legally unspecified. It does include state acts, but it is uncertain if, say, UN actions (like those in Somalia of 1993) or acts by a non-governmental organisation (NGO) such as those of a multi-national business corporation, count as external interference. Finally, there is controversy over the internal aspect of political self-determination in addition to this external dimension. What was fundamentally at issue was whether a people were fully self-determined under any system of government within an independent state or only under a liberal-democracy. (More recently the emphasis of internal self-determination has been placed on the protection of internal minorities).[5] As far as the non-political side of self-determination is concerned what counts as freely pursuing economic, social and cultural self-development is not laid down in any legal document, though the interpretation of this provision in the practices of newly independent, Third World states is instructive. On the whole and until fairly recently, they have taken it to mean the pursuit of anti-imperialist, socialist policies of development, including the Marxian variants, which go by such names as 'Arab socialism' and 'African socialism'.[6] Again, what counts as external interference in this context is somewhat vague and indeterminate. Not only are the acts of other states counted, but also those of NGOs such as the International Monetary Fund, the World Bank and multinational business corporations, among others. In addition there are the still more shadowy entities of international capitalism — Coca-Cola cultural imperialism and so forth. A final point about the legal definition of the non-political aspect of self-determination: why it should be restricted to development policies, rather than including all policies pursued by the government of an independent state, is unclear, since all policies are capable of either being freely pursued or of being subjected to external interference and constraint.

National self-determination in international law is conceptually rather messy and to some extent morally irrelevant. Accordingly, I propose to reformulate its subject and scope as follows: firstly, it will be treated as applicable to nations as well as to peoples and, secondly, its scope will be such that a people or nation will be self-determined if it is subject only to self-legislated laws, or at least to such laws — like European Community directives — which are legally self-imposed. This presupposes an independent legislature and hence (or so it seems to me) an independent, sovereign state. Claims made by jurists that the required degree of political autonomy for the nation is attained in associate statehood (e.g. the Cook Islands), or as a component of a federal state, are unconvincing as such bodies are invariably subject to some external interference or constraints, however minimal. If the political self-determination of a nation implies nothing short of independent sovereign statehood, then, such a state need not be a democracy. Internal self-determination is achieved when the nation freely chooses the political system for the independent nation-state, and democracy is only one of several options; it is possible for a nation to be subject only to its own laws, i.e. to no externally imposed ones, without having a democratic political system. Sparta was no less $\alpha\upsilon\tau o\nu o\,\mu o\sigma$ than democratic Athens. All that is necessary is that it has an apparatus for making choices and taking decisions — a national government — with the ability to act upon its decisions through its members, either through them all or through the official few who act in place and on behalf of them all collectively. It will also be assumed that internal self-determination as the protection of minorities is inapplicable unless it is either self-imposed by a majority (a later argument implies this is optional) or else the exercise of self-determination by a minority nation. Protection of minorities is otherwise a derogation from external self-determination of the majority nation; it will be externally imposed or heteronomous. Finally, there is the policy dimension of national self-determination. This is the ability of a nation to pursue its own economic, social, cultural and other policies through its own system of government, unconstrained by other states, NGOs or any other external agencies. In other words, the free pursuit of policies implies that all the constraints involved are legally self-imposed, which is to say that the nation is subject only to its own, self-legislated laws.

On this vulgarised Kantian theory, the free/self-determined nation is one which directs all its own affairs and whose circumstances are the products of an untrammelled national will expressed through the medium of law. Unlike the legal version, this concept of national self-determination recognises the nation's freedom-as-autonomy as the central moral value in nationalism. Moreover, it corresponds much more closely than the legal version to the concept of individual self-determination. The legal concept does however indicate why the

69

existence of a moral right of national self-determination is highly dubious.

In international human rights law, the self-determination of peoples is a collective or group right, that is, one which is separate and distinct from individual rights. This concept of rights presupposes the idea of legal personality, that is, a capacity to bear legal rights and duties and to have the legally constituted, corporate apparatus for acting upon them; an internal decision-making structure. The *universitas/persona moralis* is, in other words, a legally organised body and this artefact of law with its artificial personality exists only within a legal system. These considerations seem to be relevant when confronting the issue of self-determination as a collective moral right, a right attributed to national groups. If it is implausible to suggest that nations are natural corporations with natural or non-legal personalities, it is difficult to see how they can be the bearers of a moral right, especially of an active one. In the absence of a determinate internal decision-making structure, of that minimal degree of institutional organisation by virtue of which the acts of office holders can be attributed to the whole body, a nation is what Hegel termed, "a formless mass" or "an indefinite multitude".[7] In other words, it is an entity which is incapable of any kind of action, including that of self-determination. Nations, on this reading, would be aggregates of individuals who happen to have some shared characteristic/s, such as a common language or a shared religion, a common culture or a common ethnicity, a shared past or shared sentiments of solidarity and so on. In short, they would be mere collections and so incapable of exercising or bearing any kind of right whatever. Furthermore, a moral right could not be ascribed to such collections of individuals given that their shared characteristic/s is an empirical and not a moral fact. Such facts can never create moral rights. In these cases therefore the provision of an institutional apparatus for action — including that needed for self-determination — is not the concession of a moral right, but a gift of what may turn out to be morally desirable.[8] Before considering that issue it may be noted that these objections to the attribution of a collective moral right to nations are inapplicable to colonies, mandated and trust territories, etc., because all these groups are legal corporations with a more-or-less rudimentary apparatus of collective action. As such, they could in principle become moral personalities, capable of bearing moral as well as legal rights and duties. But since the concern of this essay is with nations and not with those legal personalities called 'peoples' in international human rights law, it is appropriate now to turn to the question of the moral desirability of national self-determination.

Four lines of argument will be considered: First, the instrumental justification of self-determination offered in the UN Charter (1945) and later on in meetings of the UN General Assembly, namely, that national self-determination promotes peace and justice. Second, and relatedly, the nationalist's claim that national self-determination is instrumentally and intrinsically desirable on account of its connection with human freedom. Mill's equation of the principle of national self-determination with the principle of democracy permits a third kind of justification since democracy is normally regarded as morally justifiable. Finally, there is a moral justification of national self-determination in terms of individuals, their identities and interests. Two versions of this philosophical argument will be examined. One justifies national self-determination in terms of respect for persons, the other by its service to individual well-being, that is, by its instrumental value.

## II

Before being converted into a legal human right in international law during the 1960s, self- determination had been a political principle used to reorganise the international system at the end of the First World War to promote international peace. That same eirenic purpose was explicitly stated in connection with its inclusion in the first article of the UN Charter. Subsequently self-determination was justified as a means of eliminating unjust/oppressive colonial rule and related injustices, thereby restoring human dignity to colonial peoples. Justice and peace are intrinsic goods. What is at issue is whether in fact they are promoted by self-determination.

In the case of international peace, the historical evidence to date points to an opposite result to that intended by implementing the principle of self-determination; old animosities are inflamed, existing tensions and conflicts are exacerbated and new national grievances are created, rather than international peace being fostered. Events during the past two years (1992-93) in the former state of Yugoslavia, for example, are not untypical in the pursuit of national self-determination. Given these are the facts, it follows that self-determination is morally undesirable, at least in this respect. Moreover, there is some reason for supposing these facts of history are not accidental.

Nations are self-determined to the extent that they are not subject to externally imposed constraints. But as the world of nations is a shared, social one such external constraints are unavoidable. Compromises between nations are one way in which they can be imposed and a self-determining nation will therefore not make them. Instead, it will strive to determine its own circumstances entirely, including those which it shares with other nations. Unless the nations involved are unanimous in these matters, the self-determination of one must be at the expense of the others. Since unanimity is unlikely, if all nations pursue self-determination they will inevitably be drawn into conflict with one another (for example, over territory). National self-determination is a zero sum game in a shared social world.

Against this conclusion it might be said that the true value of the self-determination of peoples lies in removing oppressive foreign rule (tyranny) and cognate injustices, rather than in some erroneously assumed eirenic propensity.

Oppression and connected injustices are, however, contingent features of foreign rule; it is, for example, perfectly possible for every human right to be respected by foreign rulers and for the violations of them by such governments to be rectified within the system of alien rule. (To assert that foreign rule is oppressive/unjust *per se* is just another way of claiming there is a moral right of self-determination which has been withheld.) Any wrongs done by a non-national government can thus be legitimately rectified, for example, by at least removing from office those individuals responsible for the wrong (as of General Dyer following the Amritsar massacre of 1919): elimination of foreign rule as such is unnecessary. In such circumstances, self-determination appears to be an inefficient means to the intrinsic good of rectificatory justice and, to that extent, less than desirable. It would be completely undesirable if its implementation removed foreign rule only to substitute an oppressive indigenous rule or, similarly, if the rectification of current injustices was achieved by merely replacing them with new, national wrongs. The relevant historical evidence points both ways, however; sometimes injustices are removed and at other times they are created by the implementation of self-determination. There is no conclusive answer to the question of its moral desirability on this line of argument then.

## III

To be subject to its own self-imposed laws within an independent state, and not to be subject to the laws or the will of another party, is what nationalists mean by the freedom of the nation. Despite its Kantian resonance, this idea of freedom is a very old one. The citizens of Sparta lived highly regimented, unfree lives, and yet proclaimed themselves to be free since they lived under their own Spartan law. A similar combination of group freedom, or the self-determined nation in an independent state, with lack of personal freedom is a feature of the present world. Amin's Uganda is only a notorious example. Equally obvious is the opposite combination of personal freedom with the absence of a free or self-determined nation, the Bretons being a case in point. Then again, there are many examples of countries where the collective and personal freedoms go together. The point is simply that there is no necessary connection between the two. This is due partly to the nature of collective/corporate rights, liberties and duties, namely, that they are logically separate from those of their individual members. So, for example, the very existence of a corporation (like a university) could be abolished by law without the civil liberties of its individual members being affected in any way. Partly also it is because different concepts of freedom are involved at the group and individual levels. Individuals enjoy what Locke called civil liberty when they are not subject to the arbitrary will of another person/s, but only to the law. These laws need not be enacted by the citizens for the condition of civil liberty to obtain. What is required is that governments, like everyone else, are subject to them. Nations, by contrast, are free when not only are they not subject to an external will, but also when laws to which they are subject are self-legislated or otherwise self-imposed. Moreover, while the nation must be subject to these laws to be free, its government need not be so bound. In other words, a fully free or independent nation-state is not necessarily a constitutional (or rule-of-law) regime. And a national government which rules unconstitutionally (or tyrannically) is one which denies the civil liberties of individual citizens. There is a third reason why national and personal freedom are not necessarily connected — the nature of self-government. If a free individual is someone who is self-governed or not ruled by others, a free nation, analogously, is one which is self-governed, not externally ruled. National and individual self-government are not, however, exact analogues. Government and the governed are identical in the case of the free or self-governing individual, but in the case of a free or self-governing nation there is no such identity; one part of the nation's membership rules the remainder. There is therefore no inconsistency between a nation's government ruling oppressively by denying the freedom of all the other members of the nation and the nation itself being free because it is self-governing.

In the absence of a necessary connection between the freedom of the nation and personal liberty, an instrumental justification of the former in terms of the latter is ruled out. Other versions of an instrumental moral justification for national self-determination have not of course been excluded, and in the final section another version will be considered, but for the moment what is important to bear in mind is that excluding the freedom version of the instrumental justification of national self-determination has no bearing on the possibility of justifying it as intrinsically morally desirable in terms of freedom. Freedom is normally regarded as an intrinsic moral good and this is accepted. For the purposes of this argument it will also be allowed that self-determination — in the sense of subjection to self-imposed laws and the pursuit of self-willed ends — where the nation is the 'self' in each case, counts as freedom. It appears then that the conclusion about its intrinsic moral desirability is inescapable. But admitting that national self-determination counts as freedom, and that freedom is an intrinsic good, does not dispose of the matter. This is because freedom in this sense is purely formal and by virtue of its vacuity is incompatible with collective rational conduct on the part of the nation. Given that rationality is a necessary feature of moral conduct, its invariable absence from the pursuit of national self-determination entails that this form of self-determination (at least) cannot be intrinsically morally desirable. This is a highly controversial claim and the argument for it is as follows.

On nationalist doctrine, a nation is free when the only laws to which it is subject are self-legislated, when its actions are exclusively in pursuit of self-willed ends and when the only constraints by which it is bound are self-imposed. By this purely formal principle of freedom no particular laws are specified, nor are any ruled out; any rule whatsoever becomes a law once the nation imposes it on itself through legislation. Similarly, no particular acts are excluded and nor are any included on this formal criterion; if the only legitimate or free actions of the nation are those in pursuit of self-willed ends, the free or self-determined nation can undertake any act or pursue any policy. On the same criterion, any possible constraint may in principle be self-imposed. However, a choice of policies and rules must somehow be made from among the many possibilities and implemented, otherwise the nation will not be self-determining. But the problem is: how? To follow the preferences of the individual members of the nation; the customary, formal rules of international law; the will of God; the principles of utility and equality or any other substantive or formal criterion, is debarred on the grounds of heteronomy. (So, far example, if a nation in asserting its claim to self-determination is required to respect an equal claim to self-determination on the part of other nations it is, to that extent, unfree, because subject to an externally imposed rule.) All substantive principles, rules or criteria, and all formal criteria, except the principle of freedom, are external to the nation, and a nation is no longer self-determined if it follows them. To circumvent this fundamental difficulty it may be suggested that a heteronomous rule could be selected by the nation and imposed by it upon itself, thereby maintaining its own autonomous status. Policy choices made by applying this rule would also be free and informed, that is, fully autonomous. But before it can be self-imposed the substantive or formal criterion must be selected by the nation and the problem is, how is that choice to be made? If it is not to be a purely arbitrary choice it must be made on some criterion or other which is not itself heteronomous. Unless the criterion is internal to the nation, using it to select a rule of conduct will not be a free act. The only criterion of choice of which this is true, however, is the formal criterion of freedom; no other formal criterion and no substantive criterion is autonomous (i.e. internal to the nation).[9] Thus both the formal and the substantive principles of choice and action must be ruled out. In their absence it follows that the formal criterion of national freedom leads ineluctably to arbitrary choices; it excludes and includes no policy, no rule and no constraint, and therefore anything adopted is necessarily criterionless or adopted arbitrarily. In effect, this is to claim that it is impossible for the actions of a self-determining nation to be rational (= non-arbitrary) and, since rationality is an essential feature of the good, such actions are not morally desirable. National self-determination as a condition of freedom is not, then, an intrinsic good, but this point can be put in another, and more succinct, way. National self-determination is intrinsically morally undesirable because its logical terminus is an unqualified national egoism.

**IV**

National self-determination is often thought to be morally desirable because it is confused with democracy and because democracy is normally assumed to be morally desirable on both instrumental and non-instrumental grounds. Indeed, in Mill's formulation of them, the two principles are equivalent statements: "When the sentiment of nationality exists in any force, there is a prima facie case for uniting all the members of the nationality under the same government, and a government to themselves apart. This is merely saying that the question of government ought to be decided by the governed."[10] But this is not to say the same thing at all, for the membership of the nationality is not identical to the category of the governed. Thus democratic principles are not being applied inconsistently when a democratically elected government denies independent statehood to a minority nation within that democracy, as the French and Spanish governments have done in the case of the Basques. Mill's fallacy may be put in another way: popular sovereignty is the democratic principle, its nationalist counterpart is the principle of national sovereignty, but since one and the same group is designated by the terms 'people' and 'nation', the two principles are only nominally different. National self-determination, on this argument, is the same as popular self-government, so if one is morally desirable the other must be too. In a democratic context, however, the 'people' and 'nation' are identical in meaning only when the group they denote is the citizen body and here self-determination is simply the exercise of state sovereignty by the citizens through their elected government. This, of course, has nothing to do with nationalism. Alternatively, if the word 'nation' denotes an ethnic, cultural or solidarist group within a state, this type of group cannot be sovereign as the citizen body of which they are a segment is so already and sovereignty is not divisible.

A final reason for rejecting any conflation of the nationalist principle with the democratic one relies on the crucial distinction between the identity of a corporation and the identities of its individual members. Not only are the rights and duties of a corporation separate from those of the individual members and non-distributive among them, but corporate acts are also not reducible to the actions of the individual members. The nationalist principle of self-determination is concerned with implementing a single, collective will — the corporate will of the nation. The democratic principle, by contrast, is concerned with implementing the wishes of individual members of that nation, among others, that is, with implementing the manifold wills of the populace. It is worth noting that the phrase, 'the will of the people', in liberal-democratic discourse (excluding Rousseau and his followers), does not refer to an indivisible corporate will, but to an aggregate of individual wills which divides into a majority and minority. Not only is it possible that a democratic decision of the populace differs, maybe even conflicts, with a volition of the collective national will, then, but also the same may be true of a democratic decision by a part of the populace, namely, the individual members of the nation in question. Our commitment to democracy as a legitimate form of government therefore entails no commitment to the nationalist claim to self-determination. If national self-determination is morally desirable at all, then it is so independently of the admitted moral desirability of democracy.


## V

The final line of argument for the moral desirability of national self-determination to be considered is in terms of individuals, their identities and their interests. It has two forms. On the first version of the argument, it is claimed that the distinctive life and character of a nation forms an important element in the personal identity of its individual members. Their identity is, to some extent, constituted by their membership of the nation; they are 'contextual individuals'. On the Kantian ideal of respect for persons, their nation ought also to be respected, most importantly by ensuring its continued existence through statehood/political independence. In essence, this is Neil MacCormick's case for an independent government for Scotland within a federal Europe.[11] It is vulnerable to at least two significant objections.

Firstly, it is an obvious *non sequitur* that respect for nations implies their organisation into separate states with separate governments. Families and religious communities are also groups the membership of which forms an important part of an individual's personal identity and which may therefore be deserving of respect. Yet it would be absurd to suggest they should be invested with the attributes of statehood, such as compulsory membership and sovereign authority over the members, in order to gain that respect from non-members. Statehood is neither implied by respect for the family nor for the faith. Respect for nations (as for families and religious communities) out of respect for persons who are their members minimally requires that the state protect them from attacks as it protects the persons of their individual members. And it is by no means self-evident that, while family groups and religious communities can be protected by and within an existing state, the same is also not true of nations. The idea that nations can only be secured in all circumstances by being organised as independent states is an extra, hidden and empirically dubious, premise of the argument.

So far it has been assumed that nations, like families and religious communities, ought to be respected. That assumption should not go unquestioned, however. Whether or not these different groups merit that respect cannot be determined collectively and *a priori*; it is an open question which can only be settled by investigating the facts of each individual case. Thus if it is admitted that a normal family deserves our respect, a family in which (say) children or the elderly were abused and exploited would not deserve respect. Similarly, a religious community the rituals of which included human sacrifice or one which practised 'brainwashing' on its members would not merit respect either, no matter how 'embedded' were its members. In both examples, a Kantian respect for persons may require their protection from the group of which they are members and, to that extent, a withholding of respect for it. This conclusion seems equally applicable to nations. A further reason why respect for persons need not mean respect for the nation of which they are members is that nations are only one of several groups which are constitutive of the sense of personal identity of their members and some other groups may, in certain circumstances, be respected (derivately) only by withholding respect for the nation. Mac-Cormick lists several such 'significant communities' — families, schools, workplace communities, religious groups, political associations, sports clubs — in addition to nations.[12] Two of them (at least) are incompatible with nations in the sense that respecting them may require withholding respect from the nation. Citizenship, for example, forms a significant part of the sense of personal identity of 'contextual individuals'. If, however, the state from which this citizenship is derived is not a nation-state in the strict sense, then respect for the nation requires withholding respect from this (? multi-national) state, and vice versa. Moreover, there is no good reason why respect for persons in such circumstances should require respect for the nation rather than for the state; only an *a priori* nationalist principle which invariably gives priority to the nation seems in its favour. Prioritising the nation is not warranted, for it presupposes that the identity of the nation is reducible to the personal identities of its members (or, at least, to the important part of those personal identities), such that respect for persons requires respect for the nation before any other 'significant community'. Such a presupposition is inconsistent with the corporate character of nations which is implied by the concept of national self-determination. Another 'significant community' which is a potential competitor to the nation for respect is the religious one. As cultural, ethnic or solidarist groups, nations are secular entities[13] and so the sense of personal identity and selfhood or character in their members of which they are constitutive is correspondingly secular. Membership of a religious community on the other hand is constitutive of an antithetical, spiritual sense of personal identity and character. Respect for persons who are members of both kinds of 'significant communities' may require making a choice between respecting the nation or the religious community, depending on the relative priority given to the secular and spiritual aspects of personal character and sense of identity. The need to make such a choice is illustrated in the following passage: "Though I am a Hellene by speech, yet I would never say I was a Hellene, for I do not believe as the Hellenes believed. I should like to take my name from my Faith, and if anyone asked me what I am I answer 'Christian'." [14] Respect for persons here clearly requires respecting this person as a Christian, not as a Greek. It is not the case then that respect for persons necessarily requires respect for the nation of which they are members. Sometimes respect for persons may require withholding it from the nation and respect for other 'significant communities', out of respect for persons who are their members, may also require respect for the nation is withheld.

In the other, non-Kantian, version of the liberal philosophical argument, the distinctive life and character of the nation is said to form an important element in the self-identity and well-being of its members and this link between the two is at the heart of the moral case for national self-determination.[15] Moreover, unlike the previous Kantian version, the corporate character of nations is central to the argument; Margalit and Raz insist that, "group interests cannot be reduced to individual interests" and that the group may therefore flourish without the lot of its members improving, and vice versa.[16] Although there is a non-reductive and indirect conceptual connection between the two, they say that, "there is no a priori way of correlating group interest with that of its members or of other individuals."[17] In some circumstances it follows an individual's well-being will be derived from that of the nation of which he is a member. In some further set of circumstances that national well-being will be secured and promoted by independent statehood for the nation while in some others it is better secured that way. In a certain combination of circumstances it follows that there is a case for national self-determination (or self-government). What those circumstances are, however, is left completely undetermined and the same is true of a consideration of the interests of non-national individuals and of the non-national interests of members of the nation which, argue Margalit and Raz, qualify the case for self-determination.[18] The case for self-determination is distinguished from the right to it, which is the right of nations (understood as cultural groups) to decide whether or not to become self-governing within a given territory, regardless of whether the case for self-determination, based on its benefits, has been established or not.[19] That right, they argue, is grounded on the importance of membership of the nation to the lives and well-being of its members, which is to say, on its instrumental value.[20]

The Margalit/Raz argument is open to exactly the same objection as the Kantian version. Allowing that nations as cultural groups are important to the lives and well-being of their members is no more a ground for a right to opt for statehood than it is in the case of families or religious communities. At the very least they would need to show that nations are of pre-eminent importance to the lives and well-being of their members in comparison with all other kinds of group to which they also belong such as a religious community, family, state and market. They merely assert that this is the case. A second criticism relates to the way in which the right is formulated by Margalit and Raz. They say that the nation which forms a substantial majority in a territory has the right to determine whether that territory shall form an independent state, but both geographical territory and nationhood are highly problematical concepts. Territories are either fixed by international law or by nature. A legally defined territory as the unit for decision-taking may be exactly what a nationalist objects to. For example, the will of the Protestant majority in the territory of the province of Northern Ireland is not regarded as morally binding by many Irish nationalists, partly because in their view the province is an artificial entity. The true territory is the natural or geographical territory of the island of Ireland. But this claim is vulnerable to the counterclaim that the true natural territory is that entire group of offshore islands called the British Isles, of which the island of Ireland is one. There is no way of resolving such a conflict of claims about the natural boundaries of territories, or of choosing between the claims made for legal and natural territories. Yet the Margalit/Raz position presupposes that territories are self-evident or uncontested units. Their concept of nations also creates major difficulties. Firstly, Margalit and Raz treat them exclusively as cultural groups, thereby excluding the alternative possible identities as ethnic and solidarist groups. This they do for no apparent reason other than perhaps that these alternative conceptions of the nation do not seem to allow their argument about the tie between its well-being and that of its individual members. If ethnic and solidarist groups are counted as nations — as they are by nationalists — there will be different and inevitably conflicting criteria of nationality. A group which counts as a nation on (say) cultural criteria may be deemed part of some other nation on (say) ethnic criteria, and there is no way in which this conflict of criteria can be decided. The result is indeterminacy. Allowing nations to be specified only as cultural groups might appear to circumvent this outcome: in fact it does not. There is still a problem of indeterminacy because culture groups have numerous characteristics which, if employed as criteria of nationality, generate conflicting results. Are the Protestants of Ulster a distinct and separate cultural nation, a segment of the Irish one or a part of a British cultural nation? The answer depends whether the cultural criterion of nationality chosen is language, folk-culture, religious tradition or history. Or again, are Germany and Austria two separate nations with strong cultural affinities, as the German Christian Democrat Party believes, or are all Germans and Austrians members of a single cultural nation, as the Austrian Freedom Party claims? The problem of the membership of a nation has no determinate solution even when the nation is treated as a self-defining group, as Margalit and Raz recommend. Membership of the nation, they say, is to be established through mutual recognition of members on the basis of shared general characteristics,[21] but since those characteristics are all cultural the indeterminacy of membership remains; different cultural criteria will be used to arrive at different memberships for the same nation. Given this indeterminacy of membership, in conjunction with that of territory, it does not seem reasonable to permit the nation, "which forms a substantial majority in a territory to have the right to determine whether that territory shall form an independent state", as Margalit and Raz contend.[22] Or, to put the point in another way, their instrumental justification of the right does not appear to be well-founded. In the first place this is because the right of self-determination is instrumentally justified, "as the method of implementing the case for self-government, which itself is based on the fact that in many circumstances self-government is necessary for the prosperity and dignity of encompassing groups [i.e. nations]",[23] when the case for self-government is itself indeterminate because it depends on circumstances which are indeterminate (see above). This indeterminacy, in conjunction with the indeterminacy of territory and nation, seems to be a recipe for envenomed disputes, chaos and conflict over both territory and membership and for that reason (instrumentally) morally undesirable.

## VI

So far then no good reason for supposing that national self-determination is morally desirable has been found, and as the usual reasons offered in its support have now been considered the conclusion must be that it is not so. It is accepted that there may be other arguments in its favour of which the author is unaware and his own treatment of those with which he is familiar is by no means invulnerable to criticism and counter-argument. Furthermore, a critical evaluation of the moral case for national self-determination which omits a full consideration of the weakest component of that case — the idea of national identity — is, to that extent (at least), deficient. In self-defence it is pleaded that this forms a very large topic which requires separate examination elsewhere.[24]

### Notes

1.   P. Sieghart: *The Lawful Rights of Mankind. An Introduction to the International Legal Code of Human Rights* (Oxford, 1986), pp. 162-3.
2.   For example, in the United Nations Charter (1945) Articles I/ii and LV; UN General Assembly Resolutions 1514 (XV)1960 "Declaration on Colonialism", 2160 (XXI)1966 and 2625 (XXV)1970 "Declaration on the Principles of International Law"; First Additional Protocol to the Geneva Conventions of 1949 (Article I/iv) 1977.
3.   The point is discussed in R. Higgins: *The Development of International Law Through the Political Organs of the United Nations* (Oxford, 1963), p. 104. See also, J. Crawford (ed.): *The Rights of Peoples* (Oxford, 1988), pp. 168-174 and H. Wilson: *International Law and the Use of Force by National Liberation Movements* (Oxford, 1988), pp. 79-88.
4.   The right to internal self-determination is currently concerned mainly with the legal protection of minority groups within the state against discrimina-

tion, internal colonialism etc. See, J. Crawford, "Outside the Colonial Context" in W.J. Allan Macartney (ed.): *Self-determination in the Commonwealth* (Aberdeen, 1988) pp. 13-14. I am grateful to Holly Cullon of the Law Faculty of the University of Hull for drawing my attention to this legal development of the right to internal self-determination.

5.  S. Neil MacFarlane: *Superpower Rivalry and Third World Radicalism: the Idea of National Liberation* (London, 1985), pp. 44-54.

6.  The distinction between the two concepts of "nation" is carefully drawn by P. Gilbert, "Criteria of Nationality and the Ethics of Self-Determination", *History of European Ideas*, 16 (4-6) 1993, pp. 516-518.

7.  G.W.F Hegel: *The Philosophy of Right* trans. Knox (Oxford, 1952), p. 183.

8.  A more extensive consideration of the claimed moral right of national self-determination is given in my paper, "The Right of National Self Determination", *History of European Ideas*, 16 (4-6), 1993, pp. 507-513.

9.  This argument assumes that nations are ethnic, cultural or solidarist groups and that there is no good reason for supposing their national characteristics are invariably of the same kind and necessarily morally desirable. For an alternative view of nations as moral communities see, P. Gilbert, "Criteria of Nationality", pp. 519-520.

10. J.S. Mill: *Utilitarianism, Liberty, Representative Government* (London, 1910), pp. 360-361.

11. N. MacCormick, "Nation and Nationalism", in *Legal Right and Social Democracy* (Oxford, 1982), pp. 247-264 and, "Is Nationalism Philosophically Credible?" in, W. Twining (ed.): *Issues of Self-Determination* (Aberdeen, 1991), pp. 8-19. My first objection to MacCormick's position is indebted to Gordon Graham's argument in, *Politics in its Place. A Study of Six Ideologies* (Oxford, 1986), pp. 137-140.

12. MacCormick, "Is Nationalism Philosophically Credible", pp. 16-17.

13. Religion sometimes features in nationalist doctrine where it is represented as an epiphenomenon, never as constitutive, of the nation. Thus, for example, "In Zionism, Judaism ceases to be the raison d'être of the Jew, and becomes, instead, a product of Jewish national consciousness." E. Kedourie: *Nationalism* 4th ed. (Oxford, 1993), p. 71. A similar secularising of Islam in Arab nationalism is examined in, S.G. Haim (ed): *Arab Nationalism* (Berkeley, 1962) pp 34-61, e.g. "Mohammad has become the founder of the Arab Nation, and Islam itself is the incarnation of the Arab national spirit." p. 56

14. Kedourie, *Nationalism*, ibid. The passage quoted is from the writings of the Patriarch of Constantinople, Gennadius (d. 1468).

15. A. Margalit & J. Raz, "National Self-Determination", *The Journal of Philosophy*, LXXXVII (9) 1990, p. 444.

16.   Margalit & Raz, "National Self-Determination", p. 449.
17.   Margalit & Raz, "National Self-Determination", p. 450.
18.   Margalit & Raz, "National Self-Determination", p. 455.
19.   Margalit & Raz, "National Self-Determination", p. 454
20.   Margalit & Raz, "National Self-Determination", p. 456.
21.   Margalit & Raz, "National Self-Determination", pp. 445-446. They admit their criteria of nations are imprecise and incapable of providing "operational legal definitions", but justify them as picking out the features of nations which "may explain the value of self-determination", pp. 447-448. Exactly such an operational definition of the nation is needed to *determine* its membership.
22.   Margalit & Raz, "National Self-Determination", p. 457.
23.   Margalit & Raz, "National Self-Determination", p. 460.
24.   See D. Miller, "In Defence of Nationality", pp. 15-32 earlier in this volume, for a sympathetic analysis of many of the issues involved.

# 6 Nationalism, liberalism and democracy

*Michael Freeman*

## 1. Nationalism and internationalism

This paper seeks to locate nationalism in the liberal-democratic tradition, where it has often lodged furtively like an illegal immigrant. I shall ask what moral significance the nation should have for liberal democrats. I shall take account of the historical association of nationalism with diverse political ideologies, but I assume for the purposes of my argument the values of liberal democracy. The puzzle I wish to address is the status of nationalism in relation to those values.

In the nineteenth century it was common for liberals and democrats to be nationalists. In the middle of the twentieth century nationalism became discredited because of its association with fascism, imperialism and war. Yet after the Second World War anti-colonial nationalism was commonly supported by liberal democrats. Recently, a diversity of nationalisms, such as those of the Baltic states, Croatia, Slovenia, Bosnia, Macedonia, Slovakia, Scotland, the Basques, the Corsicans and others have left the theory and practice of liberal democracy shell-shocked. As these dramatic developments have been taking place in the domain of political practice, the debate in political theory between "liberals" and "communitarians" has revived the "national question" in liberal-democratic theory.[1]

I wish to make a distinction between "nationalism" and "internationalism", and to this end some definitions will be useful. "Nations" can be defined objectively (by reference to common culture, history, territory, language, religion etc.) or subjectively (by reference to shared identities). For my purposes, "nations" are defined subjectively - "nations" are human collectivities who believe that they are nations - although subjective nations standardly share objective features. "Nationalism" is a doctrine that gives an especially high value or priority to the nation. "Absolute nationalism" is a doctrine that always privileges the interests of the nation of those who subscribe to it over those of other nations. "Moderate nationalism" accords value to the nation, but allows its interests to be accommodated to those of other nations and of other non-national entities (such as ethnic minorities or individuals). "Internationalism" is contrasted with "cosmopolitanism". While cosmopolitanism rejects nationalism absolutely, internationalism presupposes nationalism. Nations interact. These interactions are and should be rule-governed. Therefore there is and should be an international normative order. It follows that there is a potential conflict between international and national norms. Internationalists place a high value on international norms and are more likely than nationalists to give them priority over the interests of nations. As individuals may believe that it is sometimes right to subordinate their interests to those of others, so internationalists recognize that the interests of their nations should on occasion yield to those of other nations. Internationalism is required by the international community and by parts of the moral codes of all national communities. Thus nationalism and internationalism are not stark alternatives. Absolute nationalism rejects internationalism. But absolute nationalism is only one form of nationalism. Some forms of nationalism not only permit but also require internationalism. Yet nationalism and internationalism differ in their priorities. There is not a contradiction but there is a tension between them.

According to a not uncommon view, nations are moral communities and therefore have a primary claim on the loyalty of their members. However, this simple view is unconvincing. Many nations are morally pluralistic; some supposed nations are not moral communities at all; while others are prima facie morally outrageous. For these reasons national boundaries are not obviously moral boundaries. On the other hand, transnational relations may be morally significant. If I, carrying a plentiful supply of water, encounter a person dying of thirst in the desert, my moral relation to that person is not primarily determined by our national belongingness.

Yet simple moral cosmopolitanism is not convincing either. The nation-state may not be morally uniform but it is still the main unit of international organization. Some persons are asked to die and to kill for their country (i.e. for their nation-state), and, even if they should refuse to do so, the nation-state will loom large in the process of their refusal. For many, independently of their will, it is a morally significant other.

If it is fallacious to assume that nations are morally homogeneous, it is also fallacious to identify the nation with the state. This fallacy is embedded in international law, which treats states as the representatives of nations. International law therefore pretends to believe what everyone knows to be false. This pretence has left it largely impotent in the face of problems raised by subordinate nations. Yet states too play a moral role in contemporary politics. Individuals may be called upon to kill and to die for their states even when it is doubtful whether they represent their nations. Internationalists may hold their states accountable for their treatment of other states. Thus nations and states may constitute different moral boundaries: neither is irrelevant, neither is absolute.

It might be possible to defend the special moral status of nation-states by appeal to Edmund Burke's argument that our moral and political sentiments rise from their "natural" primary objects in the family through various secondary associations to the nation-state. Nationalists have characteristically held that the nation-state is a "natural" end-point for this process. The Burkean argument is, however, vulnerable to the objection that appeals to the putatively natural cannot settle disputes between two rival forms of social practice. Nor was Burke himself a nationalist in this sense. He was willing to appeal to the idea of the Christian civilization of Europe against the "atheists" of the French Revolution. And his commitment to natural law provided the basis of his lengthy polemic against the tyrannical practices of the British against the peoples of India. Burke was no Kantian universalist, but he was far from being a narrow nationalist.[2]

The society of nations and of states is a rule-governed community, however weakly integrated it may be. Those who support these rules also constitute a kind of community. If nations are constituted by individuals sharing certain nationalistic values, then international law and morality are constituted by norms and values which may bind individuals together in an international community. Internationalism then is not merely an indefensible over-extension of "natural" sentiments from the national to the supra-national level, but a rival commitment, in that it may evoke identities and loyalties that conflict with national obligations. These internationalist commitments are likely to be strengthened sociologically by the process of so-called globalization in transportation, communication, economies, etc. The contemporary political scene is indeed characterized by apparently contrary movements towards stronger international-ism and at the same time towards stronger nationalism.

## 2. The two faces of nationalism

David Miller has argued that nationalist beliefs are "natural" and that this fact gives them some moral weight. At the same time he acknowledges that nationalism may take forms unacceptable to the liberal democrat.[3] If we set aside for the moment the moral grounding of nationalism in its supposed naturalness, we can acknowledge that the liberal and illiberal forms of nationalism must be equally "natural". This supposed naturalistic ground does not distinguish liberal from illiberal nationalism and therefore fails a test the liberal must require. Anti-semitism is a deeply-rooted European belief but its deep historical roots cannot constitute a morally weighty ground for a liberal democrat.

Nationalism has for a long time been an embarrassment to political philosophy. It has clearly been a potent force in twentieth-century political practice throughout the world, but it does not play a central role in the principal traditions of Western theory. Its demand for collective loyalty seems to violate the liberal principle of individual autonomy. Its cross-class appeal is a considerable inconvenience to Marxism. And, if conservatism seems better able to come to terms with nationalism, we should recall the revolutionary and sometimes fairly egalitarian forms that nationalism has taken. Nationalism has not been convincingly theorized in the mainstream tradition of Western political philosophy.

Historians usually regard nationalism as a modern phenomenon, dating from the time of the French Revolution. There is some consensus that, in their origins, the idea of nationalism and that of democracy were closely related. The theoretical progenitor is Rousseau. Let us assume, with Rousseau, that the people are sovereign. Assume, with the French revolutionaries, that people = nation, and we deduce that the nation is sovereign. Set Rousseau aside in order to address problems posed by the project of attempting to democratize large societies, and we infer that the government and/or the state must "represent" the nation. Thus we have a normative ideal of the democratic nation-state. In moving from the normative political theory of Rousseau to that of the revolutionary nation-state, there is a transformation due not only to the problem of size. There is a shift from the legitimating principle of the social contract made voluntarily by consenting individuals to that of the "general will" of a people/nation committed to a shared "civil religion". This shift is manifested in an important ambiguity in the very title of the French Revolution's Declaration of the Rights of Man and of the Citizen. The Rights of Man are universalistic: they are Lockean natural-law rights inherent in every human individual. But the rights of citizens must be rights of particular citizens. In case the anti-universalistic point be missed, the Declaration locates sovereignty firmly in the nation. In the terms of our own times, the revolutionaries were not sure whether they were (universalistic) liberals or (democratic-nationalist) communitarians. The seeds of modern debates were sown.

Liberals who advocate nationalism typically draw a distinction between beneficent and maleficent nationalism. The former is required by certain positive moral and political values (e.g. by the social/national character of morality itself, by democratic citizenship) while the latter is some kind of perversion. The rise of nationalism in the French Revolution shows us how intimately interrelated these two forms of nationalism are, and helps to explain why the nice nationalist Dr Jekyll empirically so often turns into the nasty nationalist Mr Hyde. The French revolutionary concept of national citizenship was exclusionary (the poor, women and ethnic minorities were either denied or reluctantly granted citizenship), oppressive (for example, towards the speakers of non-French languages) and imperialistic. One does not have to show that democratic nationalism was a cause of these aggressive policies; it is enough that it was able, without difficulty, to justify them. Nationalism is conceptually

86

related to exclusion. The form of the exclusion is historically contingent.

Nationalism has not, of course, always been democratic. Indeed, one of its most interesting features is its ability to combine with almost any political ideology: Marxism-Leninism, democratic socialism, liberalism, conservativism, fascism, Islamic fundamentalism. Liberal democrats seeking to rehabilitate nationalism must erect very sturdy theoretical and practical barriers between illiberal and liberal nationalisms.

It is not sufficient for liberal democrats to defend the virtues of nationalism while deploring its vices, for the two are often intimately interrelated. For example, territory often plays an important part in nationalist ideology. Love of country often involves love of a particular landscape. Yet history may have inscribed a particular territory into the ideologies of more than one nation. As a consequence, attachment to the homeland, which may be expressed in music, poetry and painting, may also lead to oppression and destructive war against supposed alien intruders. The positive side of nationalism may lie in its capacity to give meaning and value to the lives of the nation. The value of nationalism may therefore be grounded in the universal human need to construct a meaningful and valuable life. But identity implies difference; inclusion implies exclusion. The positive side of nationalism implies a negative side. If the nation is positively valued, the non-nation may be negatively valued. To prevent this consequence, the positive normative theory of nationalism must be supplemented by a normative theory of internationalism.

## 3. Nationalism and political philosophy

As nationalism has proved so far to be a sturdy political survivor, so it has received support from recent developments in Western political philosophy. This has come from the communitarian challenge to universalistic liberalism. It is hard to summarize this debate briefly and accurately both because the interpretation of particular theorists is problematic (this is especially true of the leading protagonist, John Rawls) and because there are important, sometimes fundamental differences among theorists who are usually thought to belong to the same "school" (so the "communitarian" Rorty supports the "liberal" Rawls against the "communitarian" critique of Sandel).[4] We can, however, draw from the debate the following pertinent questions. Can the concept of "community" be deployed to undermine the claims of universalistic liberalism?[5] Can the "communitarian" approach to political philosophy legitimate nationalism? Can a communitarian nationalism discriminate in favour of liberal-democratic against other forms of nationalism?

## 3.1 Community

The first communitarian objection to universalistic liberalism is epistemological. To see and to know, it is argued, we must look and learn from some standpoint. Without a perspective there is neither knowledge nor judgment. There is no standpoint beyond perspective.

Epistemological perspectives are linguistically constructed. Language is rooted in and expresses a form of life. Forms of life are constituted by communities. Communities are bounded. They presuppose a "we" within the boundary and a "they" without.

The epistemological argument is related to an ontological point. Liberalism is said to be committed to the myth of the natural individual. Since this individual is asocial, it has no social characteristics. Nevertheless (say the critics) this individual is supposed to have potent properties and to perform amazing feats: it can have rights, form a political society by means of a social contract, act according to the categorical imperative, and discover the principles of justice. The problem is (according to the communitarians) that this being is a fiction. As such, it cannot perform any of the operations that are supposed to legitimate a liberal polity. Ontologically, human beings are social, and therefore only the actions of such social beings can legitimate political states of affairs.

From epistemological and ontological communitarianism certain values are thought to follow. Valuing itself is a social activity. Whatever is valued or is worthy of being valued is so as part of a social process. Epistemological, social, moral, political, religious and aesthetic values are social products. This argument has radically relativistic implications. If all values (including truth-values) are both produced and validated by particular societies, then it would seem that there are no universal truths but only socially-relative truths. But this looks very much like a self-contradictory claim. Moral and political communitarians are wont to say that there is no position outside communities from which they may be judged. To sustain this position, however, it would be necessary to draw a distinction between moral and political arguments, on the one hand, and epistemological arguments, on the other, for communitarian politics seems to require an "external" validating moral epistemology. Without such an external epistemology communitarianism appears to be groundless.


## 3.2 Nation

The strong epistemological and ontological form of communitarianism is, therefore, not convincing. There remains, however, the argument that community grounds social value and is therefore itself a fundamental value. Can this argument provide a grounding for nationalism?

In sociology the concept of "community" has proved notoriously problematic. At its worst, communitarian political philosophy repeats the crudest fallacies of functionalist sociology. "Communities" are assumed to be stable, integrated systems characterized by consensus over fundamental values. There is a danger that the fiction of the natural individual is being replaced by the rival fiction of the consensual community. If "community" is to have some moral claim upon us, and we reject the fiction of the consensual community, then we shall need an alternative account of community.

In this light the claims of the communitarians are unclear. Communities are sometimes assumed to be national communities, at other times cultural communities that may be less or more than national communities, yet again a community may be constituted by any set of like-minded individuals. Thus Americans, those belonging to the Judeo-Christian tradition or cosmopolitan intellectuals might all constitute communities. However, because "we" implies "they", there can be no universal community. But the case for privileging national over other limited (including transnational) communities is not made.

David Miller has suggested that the nation-state is the most appropriate unit for democratic politics and for distributive justice. "The collective identities that people currently possess are predominantly national identities. Here, if anywhere, it seems, the promise of overall community must be redeemed."[6] There is surely a questionably rapid move from "is" to "must" here, as well as a number of questionable assumptions, viz.: (i) national identities are predominant; (ii) national identities therefore ought to be predominant; (iii) a predominant identity is normatively required by political philosophy.

Are national identities predominant? There seems to be plenty of nationalism about. But it is not obvious that national identities are the most important for the majority of the world's population. It may well be that sub-national identities predominate for many people. In many European societies the boundaries of the nation are confused. Are ethnic Hungarians in Romania Hungarians or Romanians? Are gypsies in Hungary Hungarians or gypsies?

Should national identities be predominant? Here we see the two faces of nationalism. Love of national culture and hatred of foreigners do not necessarily but do often combine. A short while ago, it is said, some Yugoslavs did not know whether they were Serbs or Croats. National identity has come, as it has so often come in history, out of the barrel of a gun. There is something to be said for having a confused identity.

Should we celebrate the idea of a predominant identity? We have been here before. Class was a predominant identity for Marxists. Gender is for feminists. Nation is for nationalists. There seems no reason to give ontological priority to a particular identity. There seem to be moral grounds for caution, since privileging particular identities in this way facilitates a Manichean view of politics: "we" versus "them". Each of these identities may be morally useful in certain circumstances. Each can be dangerous. The current fashion for nationalism is uncertain ground for its being morally appealing.

Do good fences really make good neighbours? It depends upon what is happening on the other side of the fence. Where those who are prosperous on one side of a fence fail to come to the aid of people starving on the other side, the latter are unlikely to regard the former as good neighbours. If, on one side of the fence, one person is murdering another, the neighbour who does nothing is not a good neighbour. National identities are fences and they may sometimes make good neighbours but at other times they may inhibit neighbourliness.

The defect of the old sociological idea of community was its assumption of closure. We can now see that, empirically, communities rarely have closed borders. History is a record of cultural exchange. If communities are open-textured, so are nations. If the nation is a morally and politically proper object of loyalty for some purposes, it is unlikely to be so for all. Nationalism has a bad name partly because of its quasi-totalitarian claim to loyalty.

If the nation has neither clear nor closed boundaries, there is space for trans-national moral commitments. The nation does not bound our world either of meaning or of sympathy. The boundary between fellow-nationals and non-nationals may be morally significant, but it is not exclusively so. The boundary between fellow-nationals and non-nationals may be morally significant but it is not exclusively so. Whatever may ground a theory of justice is not required to carry a passport. If nothing grounds a theory of justice, then neither does nationality.

Historians agree that the nation is a historical product. Internationalism is equally so. Thus, whether the starting-point for political philosophy is some form of neo-Kantian universalism or neo-Hegelian historicism, we have to take internationalism seriously. Burke said that there were no rights of Man, only rights of Englishmen, Frenchmen, etc. Whether or not that was true when he said it, it is not true now. The "human being" is now a moral category. The contemporary world is constituted by diverse cultures, but they are not morally independent of each other. When, in the aftermath of the war in the Persian Gulf in 1991, the Kurds appealed to the international community for assistance against the persecutions of the Iraqi state in the name of common humanity, their appeal was trans-culturally intelligible and cogent.

A traditional task of political philosophy is the search for the principles of the just organization of power. The task of democratic theory is to find viable forms of meaningful people-power. The democratic impulse has often been towards small political units so that rule is close to the people. But power rarely stays where democrats would wish it to. Markets distribute power as well as wealth. States distribute wealth as well as power. We have seen that the idea of the nation and the principle of democracy have been closely associated at certain historical moments, but that each can live without the other. Whatever the future of the nation-state, the present prospect is one of the internationalization of power. The principle of democracy will accordingly require some internationalization of community.

At the end of the twentieth century nationalism is in full cry. We cannot say now how the balance between the good and the evil it produces will be viewed in later times. We can see some of the traditional evils of nationalism clearly enough. And the case for an internationalist theory of justice seems strong. Nationalism can look after itself. The more important, and harder task for political philosophy is to develop a plausible theory of international justice. The communitarian turn in liberal and socialist theory is a turn away from an historical project that is needed now more than ever. It is theoretically flawed and practically unhelpful. There are therefore grounds for optimism that it will soon be deconstructed and transcended.

## Notes

1. David Miller: *Market, State and Community: Theoretical Foundations of Market Socialism* (Oxford: Clarendon Press, 1990), especially chapter 9. See also Michael Walzer, "The Moral Standing of States: A Response to Four Critics", Philosophy and Public Affairs, 9:3, 1980, pp. 209-229; replies to Walzer, Charles R. Beitz, "Nonintervention and Communal Integrity", Philosophy and Public Affairs, 9:4, 1980, pp. 385-391; David Luban, "The Romance of the Nation-State", 392-397; Gerald Doppelt, "Statism without Foundations", pp 398-403.
2. Michael Freeman: *Edmund Burke and the Critique of Political Radicalism* (Oxford: Blackwell, 1980).
3. David Miller, "In Defence of Nationality", pp. 15-32 earlier in this volume.
4. Richard Rorty, "The Priority of Democracy to Philosophy", in Merrill D. Peterson and Robert C. Vaughan, eds: *The Virginia Statute for Religious Freedom: its Evolution and Consequences in American History* (Cambridge: Cambridge University Press, 1988).
5. See Simon Caney, "Liberalism and Communitarianism: a Misconceived Debate", Political Studies, XL:2, 1992, pp. 273-289.
6. Miller: *Market, State and Community*, p. 238.

# 7 National identity and the ontological regeneration of Britain

*Bhikhu Parekh*

Like individuals, societies go about their daily business in a largely un-selfconscious manner. They are generally well-adjusted to their environment and have adequate resources to deal with such problems as they face. A difficult situation arises when they are confronted with unusual problems and painful choices, or when their environment undergoes rapid and extensive changes, or when their way of life faces unexpected internal or external threats. Their horizon of expectations is then disturbed, their habitual assumptions about their social world are challenged, and the tacit self-understanding upon which they normally rely proves inadequate. They feel disorientated and confused, and their conduct lacks coherence and a sense of direction. Consciously or unconsciously their members are then led to ask deeper questions about who they are, what they stand for, what values are central to their way of life, how they are changing, and if and how they should reconstitute themselves. Different societies conduct the self-examination and cope with the heightened self-consciousness in their own different ways, and build up their own distinct traditions of self-reflection.[2]

British society began to undergo significant changes from the late 1960s onwards. Thanks to the changes in the moral climate, the British people became much more open and uninhibited about their choices of life styles and sexual preferences. They not only challenged the prevailing moral consensus on how individuals should lead their personal lives, but also demanded the right to profess and practise their self-chosen life-styles without legal and social discrimination and disapproval. As a result of the decolonisation of most of the Empire, Britain's two centuries of imperial adventure came to an end, leading to a drastic shrinkage of its geographical expanse, political power, and sense of global importance. Thanks to the arrival of a large number of black and brown immigrants from the erstwhile colonies and to their concentration in the major cities, British society was becoming recognisably different and faced with problems created by the presence of "alien" cultures. The British economy was in a state of decline. Its industrial productivity was low, its technology outdated, the quality of its management poor, and its balance of payments was unfavourable. Its political institutions, widely perceived to be ineffective and commanding only limited popular support, raised the spectre of whether it was governable. The pressure from influential quarters to join the European Community generated widespread fears about the loss of its "one thousand years of history" and distinctive political identity. In short, almost all the traditional sources of pride in terms of which Britain had for several centuries constructed its collective identity — namely the Empire, social cohesion, stable democratic institutions, the industrial leadership of the world, superiority to the rest of Europe and so on — were proving problematic. Almost everyone recognised that the country faced a deep crisis of confidence and could not go on as before.[3]

Many felt enthusiastic about some of these changes and sought to incorporate them in a new vision of Britain. They welcomed its multicultural composition as well as the climate of "liberation" brought about by the new moral and social freedoms. Some of them were also highly critical of the insularity, anti-intellectualism and uncritical traditionalism of the British way of life, and looked forward to the changes likely to be brought about by its integration into Europe. They believed that both Europe and the ethnic minorities would help pluralise Britain, bring in new sources of energy, break up its class system, and make it a culturally rich and lively society. They were all, of course, deeply worried about its economic and political decline, and thought that it could be arrested by appropriately restructuring its economic and political institutions.

An increasingly influential body of people, conventionally called the New Right, took an entirely different view. They disapproved of almost all these changes. In their view the new moral and social freedoms signified a loss of shared moral values and undermined the very foundation of the British way of life. The "permissive society" — the very term was suggestive — gave no moral guidance to its members, lacked moral commitment and self-confidence, and was not a society in any intelligible sense of the term. In the New Right view, the economic decline was not caused by economic factors alone. It had deep moral roots in the loss of economically central moral virtues and values, and could not be reversed by tinkering with economic institutions and practices. This was also the case with political decline. The presence of the culturally different ethnic minorities threatened the cohesion and integrity of the British way of life, and the prospect of "joining" Europe had similar implications. In the New Right view, Britain was not just changing but declining, and that too not just in some but in all areas of life. Its comprehensive and relentless decline was caused by its loss of self-confidence and the great virtues that had once stood it in good stead, and this in turn owed its origin to the fact that Britain's national identity had become "diluted", "eroded" and "confused". Britain could only be regenerated by rediscovering and reaffirming that identity.

In this paper I intend to explore the role the idea of national identity played in the New Right political discourse, asking why it was introduced and how it was defined and deployed. Although a number of writers helped shape the New Right discourse, I shall concentrate on its two most influential advocates, namely Enoch Powell and Margaret Thatcher. In the last section I shall briefly indicate why in my view the New Right view of national identity is deeply flawed.

# I

Enoch Powell was one of the first to introduce the idea of national identity into post-Second World War British political discourse. As he put it in 1963[4]:

> I suppose few nations have had, in a single generation, to confront the fact and the effects of such tremendous changes in their world situation as Britain has had to do in the last 30 years. In so short a space of time had a globe with one quarter of the land surface coloured red, our naval and air predominance, and our commercial, industrial and financial primacy become things of the past. History is littered with nations that have been destroyed for ever by the stress of lesser changes than these. But greatness does not consist in mere size, mere power. It lies in a realistic appraisal of the true stature of a nation, neither exaggerated, nor underestimated, and a faith in the unique possibilities for the future with which our history and our position have endowed us.

Powell argued that, since Britain had undergone such massive changes in such a short time, it needed to take a cool and critical look at itself, identify its "true nature", return to its "roots" and build the future on that basis. He was not worried about the disappearance of the British Empire. In his view the imperial consciousness, manufactured by Joseph Chamberlain and used by the Conservative Party for rhetorical purposes, was basically a "hallucination" without deep roots in British self-consciousness.[5] As such its loss meant little to the country's sense of identity and self-confidence. Since the existence of the Commonwealth perpetuated the hallucination, Powell urged its dissolution or at least British withdrawal from it. As to the economic decline, he thought that it could be reversed by setting the economy free of state regulation and releasing the great British virtues of hard work, ambition and enterprise. What worried him most were the alleged dangers posed by the presence of the ethnic minorities and the prospect of Britain joining Europe, the former threatening the integrity of the British way of life from within, and the latter from outside. The dangers could not be averted unless the country fully appreciated what was at stake, and it could not do so without becoming fully conscious of its national identity. The fact that the Empire had ended and Britain was once again "rediscovering affinities with earlier generations" reinforced the need to rediscover and reaffirm its identity.

For Powell, Britain needed "more than ever" to discover and "be true" to itself, for "always throughout history, it is when Britain had been most herself that she has had most to offer."[6] It had a unique "genius or national character" which underpinned and gave inner coherence to its collective life. British national identity was a product of its long and unbroken history, and was already fixed. It made Britain a specific kind of country and formed its ontological basis. Happiness and success only came to nations "that know themselves as they really are". Unless the British people discovered their innermost "impulses" and "instincts" as revealed in their history and attained true self-knowledge, they risked losing their identity and cohesion. Since most of them were incapable of this, the responsibility to offer the nation authentic self-understanding fell on its leaders.

For Powell, British national identity lay in its institutions, values and orientation to itself and the world. Broadly speaking it had four main components. First, it involved parliamentary sovereignty. The House of Commons was "the personification of the people of Britain; its independence is synonymous with their independence." The history of Britain as a nation was integrally bound up with and uniquely expressed in the history of its Parliament, the unique focus and locus of its collective identity. Second, Britain was a fundamentally individualist society and deeply cherished the rights and liberties of the individual. This was more true of it than of any other society, and the roots of its individualism not only went as far back as the beginning of its history, but were embedded in the racial character of the British people. Third, British national identity was grounded in and constantly nurtured by the ethnic and pre-political unity of the British people. The British were a cohesive people, intensely aware of their ethnic identity and bound by deep ties of kinship and loyalty to those of their kind. They had a strong sense of "the homogenous we" and instinctively knew who were outsiders and did not belong to them. Fourth, thanks to its geography and history, British national identity was distinctly singular and unattached. Britain was an island and not a part of any continent. Its history reflected its geography and was uniquely global. For long periods of history that were crucial to its development, Britain "had stood with her face to the oceans, her back to Europe". And even when it crossed the oceans to rule the world, it never struck roots anywhere. Unlike earlier empires it did not extend its polity with its power and so compromise its singularity and integrity. Since it had always remained itself and belonged to no larger entity, it was able both to be true to itself and to remain open to the world.

Powell used his conception of British national identity to arrive at important conclusions concerning controversial political issues. He condemned the devolution of power to Scotland and Wales on the ground that it involved abdicating parliamentary sovereignty to "anti-parliaments", and destroyed both the unity and the identity of the country. Parliament was the unique focus and concentrated expression of the British national identity, and to detract from its sovereignty was to blur and weaken that identity. He condemned what he called collectivism and large parts of the welfare state because they were incompatible with British individualism and the moral virtues associated with it. He insisted that British people would never accept and assimilate the ethnic minorities because their sense of who they were instinctively revolted against the alien cultural presence. Powell therefore suggested that the ethnic minorities be repatriated and that, if this were not possible, their rights should be retrospectively reduced. He would not allow their wives and young dependents to join them and regretted his earlier advice to the contrary.

Since British national identity was singular, Powell concluded that it would be suicidal of Britain to join Europe. It was not a European nation. It was no doubt geographically close to Europe, but that was a contingent matter of no great political or cultural significance. Its history had always been enacted within its own borders and on the high seas, but not in Europe, and its cultural, political, economic and other institutions as well as pattern of historical evolution were also distinct. Casting its lot with other European nations was therefore bound profoundly to damage its identity. Powell conceded that other European states did not see the matter this way, but insisted that their identities were very different from the British. Since their democratic institutions were of more recent origin and did not have deep historical roots, they did not feel deeply attached to them. The Continental states were also quite similar to each other both because they had sprung from the Napoleonic and subsequent historical experiences and because they had a common social base in peasant agriculture. They also had similar legal and administrative institutions and shared a common outlook on politics and society. The federal idea therefore came naturally to them and did not damage their national identity. Britain was quite different from them in all significant respects.

Powell's political views on these and other matters received only limited support among the political leaders and the bulk of the British people. Even so far as the racial question was concerned, no one seriously endorsed his ideas on repatriation and curtailment of minority rights. But none of these led him to ask if his conception of British identity might not be deeply mistaken. Instead he attacked the successive British governments for being "out of touch" with the British people and not allowing the latter to express their "true feelings". As to why they did not share his fears, he blamed either their false consciousness or a conspiracy by unnamed groups within and outside the Civil Service. Although Parliament was supposed to be the linchpin of British identity, Powell did not explain how he felt entitled to challenge its collective judgement and to pit his own against it.

Even his inconsistent appeal from Parliament to the nation ran into difficulties

97

when the British people voted in a referendum to join the European Community. Powell now felt deeply disillusioned and blamed them for failing to know who they really were. Just as he had said in 1968 that the nation was fuelling its funeral pyre by admitting the ethnic minorities, he now lamented that it had "lost its will to live" and was "dying politically, or rather perhaps committing suicide'. He went on, "The people of Britain, not just passively but with apparent relish, have relaxed and enjoyed the rape of their national and parliamentary independence". They were all victims of false self-consciousness, and had either wilfully or under the influence of false fears declined his offer of true self-knowledge. He had no doubt that he was right and that he knew the British people better than they did themselves, and took solace in the belief that no messiah is ever respected in his own age.

Margaret Thatcher broadly shared the Powellite view of Britain but, since some of her concerns were different, she modified it in several important respects.[7] She was convinced that Britain had steadily declined since the 1950s in all major areas of life. She thought that this was so because it had lost its self-confidence and a sense of national purpose, and that this was due to the systematic erosion of its national identity. Britain did not know what it was and stood for, and its self-ignorance made it an easy prey to the latest ideological fashions including collectivism, culture of dependency, multiculturalism, Europeanism, cosmopolitanism and the permissive society. It needed to return to its roots and recapture the virtues and self-understanding that had once made it great. Like Powell, Thatcher argued that the British national identity was already fixed, and a product of the interaction between the racial qualities of its people and their unique historical experiences. Like him, again, she was not clear about the causes of the erosion of that identity, and tended to blame British self-forgetfulness, ignorance of history brought about by bad education, and the invasion of the collectivist and bureaucratic ideas from the continent of Europe. She was convinced that British society and character desperately needed to be regenerated, and that the only way to do so was to reconstruct them on the basis of its national identity.

Enoch Powell felt it necessary to define the British national identity because of his fears about the "great" threats posed by the presence of the ethnic minorities and the prospect of joining the European Community. Thatcher shared Powell's fear of Europe, but unlike him she knew that Britain could no longer opt out of it. She therefore could not accept his anti-European definition of British national identity, and needed so to define the latter that it was clearly distinguished but not totally disconnected from Europe. As for the presence of the ethnic minorities, she shared Powell's fears. However, she thought that he had greatly exaggerated the threat and that, in spite of some initial difficulties, British society could easily integrate them and even benefit from their, especially the Asian entrepreneurial skills and family ethics. For her a far greater threat to the British way of life came from socialism, which encouraged statism and the culture of dependency and undermined individual enterprise.

For Thatcher, Europe and socialism posed the greatest threats to British national identity. In her view the two were closely connected. For her, socialism was distinctly European in origin and had no roots in Britain, where it was an alien import deriving such legitimacy and power as it possessed solely from its European connections. She made clear that the interrelated evils of Europeanism and socialism were Britain's greatest enemies against which she had fought during her thirteen years in office in an important statement she made soon after her resignation.[8]

> I always said and believed that the British character is quite different from the characters of people on the Continent — quite different. There is a great source of fairness and equity in the British people, a great sense of individuality and initiative. They don't like being pushed around. How else did this really rather small people, from the times of Elizabeth on, go out in the larger world and have such an influence upon it? I set out to destroy socialism because I felt it was at odds with the character of the people. We were the first country in the world to roll back the frontiers of socialism, then roll forward the frontiers of freedom. We reclaimed our heritage.

Since Thatcher was led to define British national identity in the context of the twofold threat, she defined it in contrastive terms. She drew a neat contrast between Britain and Europe. Britain was what Europe was not, and vice versa. As the above quotation makes clear, for Thatcher British people were fair and equitable whereas continental Europeans were not, the British people possessed individuality and initiative whereas the Europeans were devoid of or at least deficient in them, and so on. Thatcher drew a similarly rigid contrast between British identity and socialism. Socialism was wholly Continental in origin, and Britain had nothing to do with it. Socialism stressed the value of society and praised and blamed it respectively for individual achievements and failures. By contrast, British individualism valued the individual and expected him to accept full responsibility for his character, circumstances and actions. Since Thatcher defined British individualism in contrast to Continental socialism, she defined it in lean and austere terms and squeezed out all elements that even remotely resembled socialism. Her much-quoted remark that "there is no such thing as society" is a logical consequence of this.

As Thatcher defined it, British national identity had the following components. First, Britain was a part of Europe but not a European country. Like the rest of Europe it was Christian; its language, literature, arts and architecture were influenced by Europe; for three centuries it had been part of the Roman Empire; and some of its ancestors such as the Celts, Saxons and Danes had come from the Continent. Although Britain was an heir to the European heritage, it was

99

fundamentally different from the rest of Europe. The process of its individuation began under the Norman and Angevin rule in the eleventh and twelfth centuries when it was "restructured" and embarked upon its unique and uninterrupted historical journey.[9] It developed its own distinct values, institutions, style of politics, outlook on life, and so on. And although it was always deeply involved in Continental politics, it was also a global power with deep commitments and interests in almost every part of the world. As a result Britain was "a country which has little resemblance to the rest of Europe." It could and indeed must work closely with the rest of Europe, but its European identity would always remain tangential and subordinate to, and could never dominate let alone replace its unique national identity.

Given her view of the British national identity, Thatcher took a condescending view of its relations with Europe. Although Britain had benefited from its European connections, Europe had profited far more. The Europeans were not good at managing their affairs and constantly got into a serious mess. Britain had repeatedly had to step in to save them from their follies and had been their protector and saviour at crucial moments. The distinct British identity had thus served well not only Britain but also Europe, and it was in the latter's own interest to respect and nurture it. As Thatcher put it in her important Bruges speech:[10]

> We British have in a special way contributed to Europe. Over the centuries we have fought to prevent Europe from falling under the dominance of a single power. We have fought and we have died for her freedom. Only miles from here in Belgium lie the bodies of 120,000 British soldiers who died in the First World War. Had it not been for that willingness to fight and to die, Europe *would* have been united long before now — but not in liberty, not in justice. It was British support to resistance movements throughout the last War that helped to keep alive the flame of liberty in so many countries until the day of liberation .... It was from our island fortress that the liberation of Europe itself was mounted.

For Thatcher, parliamentary democracy was the second vital component of British national identity. Like Powell, she regarded Parliament, especially the House of Commons as the basis of British political life. Britain began its history with an absolute monarchy, but its unique genius lay in pioneering and perfecting representative institutions and taming the monarchy. Its history as a nation was tied up with and embodied in the evolution of Parliament, the unique focal point of its national identity.

Third, Britain was a uniquely individualist country. The British people loved liberty above everything else, and deeply distrusted the state. Thatcher conceded that the continent of Europe too had a strong liberal tradition, but argued that it had never known how to reconcile liberty and order and uneasily oscillated between the extremes of anarchism and authoritarianism. The Continentals associated liberty with will and exercised it without regard to rules and norms. Since this led to aggression and chaos, the powerful and centralised state became necessary to create order. By contrast the British associated liberty with reason, and built into its exercise a necessary respect for others and for social and legal norms. Their liberty therefore did not create disorder and conflict, and required only a minimum intervention by the state. British political culture had developed and was centred around civic or responsible individualism, and avoided the anarchism and the correlative collectivism of the Continentals. Furthermore, although the British cared deeply about fairness, they happily did not share the Continental interest in equality. While equality led to collectivism and curtailment of liberty, fairness went hand in hand with a responsible exercise of liberty.

Fourth, for Thatcher British national identity was characterised by a distinct set of virtues. They were of three kinds: first, such economic virtues as enterprise, resourcefulness, competitiveness and the capacity to defer immediate satisfaction; second, such political virtues as patriotism, public spirit and civic participation; and third, such personal virtues as accepting responsibility for the consequences of one's actions, not being a burden on others, preferring the dignity of poverty to the indignity of public or state charity, love of the family and adherence to conventional sexual morality. For Thatcher these virtues had made Britain great in the past and were responsible for its cohesion and unity. They were central to the self-conception of the average Briton who cherished them and defined his self-respect in terms of his ability to live up to their demands. She acknowledged that the virtues had declined in recent years, but was convinced that, since they were deeply embedded in the British national character, the decline was temporary and reversible.

Finally, like Powell, Thatcher insisted that British identity had an inescapable ethnic basis. Over the centuries the different ethnic groups that came to Britain had become integrated, and the British now formed a homogeneous group. They felt bound together by strong ties of kinship and instinctively knew who belonged to them and who were outsiders. That was why they rushed to the defence of the Falklanders when the latter were attached by Argentina. Since they had a strong sense of nationhood, and since that sense was grounded in and nourished by a shared ethnic basis, they "naturally" felt threatened by the ethnic minorities. Unlike Powell, Thatcher realised that the latter could not be repatriated or deprived of their rights, and insisted that their distinct ways of life should be dismantled and their members assimilated both culturally and biologically into the British "stock'. Until that happened, they remained British *citizens* but could not be considered *British*, that is, they were members of the British *state* enjoying equal rights of citizenship, but they could not belong to the British *nation* and fully participate in its inner life.

British national identity as Thatcher defined it became the operative philosophy of her administration. It indicated to her what the British people were "essentially" like, what their deepest hopes and aspirations as well as strengths and weaknesses were, how they "really" wished their country to develop, and what "national purposes" they wanted it to pursue. This insight into the innermost nature and ontological structure of the nation provided her with an overarching conceptual framework within which she conceptualised and dealt with political issues. Her view of British national identity acted both as an anchor and a compass, giving her a sense of conviction and self-confidence as well as a sense of direction. She obviously could not *deduce* specific policies from it, for that depended on contingent circumstances. But it did give her a set of general principles for deciding what issues or aspects of a situation were significant, why and to what degree.

Her various policies and actions are too well-known to need elaboration. Since she knew that it was not in Britain's interest to leave the European Community, she insisted on so reshaping it that it became more hospitable to the preservation of British identity.[11] She wanted the Community to become a "family of nations" respecting and nurturing their distinct ways of life rather than a superstate moulding them all in the image of a single and homogeneous European identity. She demanded that it should cherish enterprise, eschew collectivist planning, drop the social charter, encourage free trade, open itself up to Eastern Europe, avoid centralisation and uniform regulations, and so on. In the ultimate analysis her central concern was both to remould the Community in the British self-image, and to use its powers to make the Continental countries more or less like the Britain of her imagination. Her subtle attempt not only to restructure the Community but also to anglicise the political and cultural life of its members was reminiscent of the British imperial mission of "civilising" the rest of the world, and aroused their deepest fears.

Domestically Thatcher devoted all her efforts to restructuring British society and regenerating the British national character on the basis of her view of its national identity. Convinced that the British people had lost the virtues required by the enterprise culture and needed to be re-educated, she turned to education as a major tool of cultural engineering. She gave the state unprecedented educational powers, including the powers to determine the content of the school curriculum, the nature and substance of teacher training, to inspect schools and universities and to intervene in their internal affairs. She took particular care that the curriculum, especially the three vital subjects of English language, history and religious education cultivated the virtues she considered central to British national identity.

The economy was another major instrument of social regeneration. Her massive programme of privatisation was designed not only to disburden the state of its economic functions and clearly to demarcate the boundaries of the state and the economy, but also to create a competitive and entrepreneurial society hospitable to the development of the kind of "vigorous" national character she desired. It had a deep cultural and moral thrust, and went hand in hand with her educational reforms. Anxious to re-establish the sovereignty of Parliament, she abolished the post-war "corporatist" or tripartist style of politics in which the government had taken important economic decisions in co-operation with industries and the trade unions. Since she thought that British national identity was basically individualist, she made individual choice one of the central organising principles of all areas of life, and dismantled or emasculated institutions suspected of nurturing socialist ideas and aspirations. She was determined that nothing should stand between the individual and the state, and that no institution should be so autonomous as to frustrate or slow down her central goal of national regeneration.

These and her other policies became highly controversial and provoked much opposition. My concern here is not to assess their merits, nor to trace their inevitably slow and hesitant evolution, nor to explore how she mesmerised the nation and broke down all opposition, but to elucidate the way in which she justified her policies to herself and to the country. For Thatcher her policies were designed to restore British national identity. Britain had a distinct genius, identity, soul or essence, and nothing that went against it was likely to succeed. She enjoyed a privileged access to and was the high priestess of national Being. For decades successive political leaders, pathetically ignorant of the national character and identity and victims of false self-consciousness, had misled the nation and passively presided over its decline. She said she was different. She knew the national soul, was in tune with its deepest stirrings, and able to work in harmony with them. All this gave her political discourse a quasi-religious character and generated a distinct mode of argumentation.

She insisted that the values inspiring her politics were neither arbitrary nor a matter of personal preference, but ontologically grounded in British national identity. As such they were objective and obligatory and admitted of no alternative. She dismissed her critics as being "out of touch" with British national character and in love with foreign ideas, and insisted that the "British people would not stand" for their policies. She did not generally feel it necessary either to argue against their ideas or to advance well-considered arguments in defence of her own. For her it was enough to insist that their ideas went against the "national grain", were inauthentic, not rooted in British character and tradition, and that by contrast her own were no more than the authentic expressions of the British soul. Her identity-based style of political discourse ruled out arguments, and largely consisted of quasi-religious pronouncements deriving their authority from her epistemologically privileged access to the national identity.

Her style of discourse gave her many rhetorical advantages. As we have seen, it spared her the trouble and the risk of answering her critics in a genuine intellectual debate. Since she appealed to British national identity rather than to universal principles, she appeared intensely patriotic and as someone whom the nation could confidently trust to pursue its interests. She was also able to evoke deep historical memories and a sense of national pride. Since she said that she was only concerned to retrieve those values and virtues that had once made the country great, she aroused hopes for a similar future. In appealing to national identity and asking her countrymen not to betray their ancestors, she was also able to mobilise the sentiments of ancestral loyalty and fuse her stress on the individual and the national family in a highly potent political symbiosis. The elements of rebuke, guilt and even moral blackmail that this involved carried a considerable psychological force.

## II

I have so far sketched the basic features of the Powellite and especially the Thatcherite political discourse and the role played in it by the idea of the British national identity. The discourse was deeply flawed.

The very concept of national identity is deeply problematic. Every society consists of several subcultures and ways of life based on the differences of gender, region, religion, class and so on. To suggest that it has a single way of life is to ignore these diversities and to impose on them an artificial unity. It is, of course, true that a society needs a common mode of conducting its collective affairs. But that is limited to and not needed outside its shared political life. The unity of a society lies in its shared political institutions and culture, and the latter not only can and do easily coexist with but also often protect and nurture diversity in other areas of life. The unity of a society therefore is necessarily partial and limited, and can never encompass all aspects of its life as Thatcher and the New Right imagined. To think otherwise and to imagine that political life needs to be based on a pre-political foundation is to confuse state with society, to politicise all areas of life, and to give the state a wholly illegitimate and dangerous right to reshape society in its own image.

The distinctiveness or individuality of a society then lies in its political institutions and culture, that is, in its *political* way of life. By its very nature the latter is highly complex and fluid, a historically developed and inherently delicate balance of different and even conflicting tendencies. No society exists or develops in isolation from the rest and every society necessarily shares several elements in common with others, which it no doubt integrates with its other features in its own unique manner. A way of life is distinct, but neither closed nor capable of being neatly demarcated from others. When one uses the language of *identity* rather than *individuality*, one runs the risk of missing out this vital point. One tends to reify, essentialise and homogenise a way of life, ignore its fluidity, suppress its points of similarity and overlap with others, and to freeze its further development. However, it does not matter how one defines the term identity as long as one appreciates that it is not homogenous, static and

104

exclusive.

It is precisely this that Thatcher, Powell and the New Right in general ignored. They took what I might call a realist or substantialist view of national identity. For them, British national identity was historically determined, a brute and unalterable fact of life, and passively inherited by each generation. All one could do is to acquire an authentic understanding of it and remain true to it. This view is false and refuted by the historical experiences of every known community. The national identity is not a homogeneous substance like the Christian soul, but a cluster of different and relatively open-ended tendencies and impulses developed at different times and in response to different situations. Each generation defines, interprets, develops and balances them differently and modifies them in the light of its needs and circumstances. National identity is therefore both inherited and constantly reconstituted. To be true to it is not to treat it as sacred and inviolable, but to creatively relate it to and reconstruct it in the light of changing circumstances. Since national identity is a product of history, as Thatcher herself admitted, it can also be unmade and remade in history — unless one naively assumes that history somehow came to an end at a particular point in time.

Thatcher also made the mistake of treating national identity as if it were transparent and coherent. National identity is a precipitate of many different influences, and includes a host of disparate and dimly grasped elements that are often too deep or fluid to be accessible to self-consciousness. Since one is deeply shaped by it, one also necessarily lacks the distance to view it from the outside. National identity can therefore never be fully and unambiguously articulated, and any claim to enjoy a privileged access to it is fraudulent. It is a cluster of different and uncoordinated tendencies developed over the course of a long history, and is by its very nature messy and incoherent.

Since national identity is necessarily complex, multi-layered and incoherent, every attempt to define it involves abstracting a specific aspect of it. In so doing one not only misses out its other aspects, but also distorts those one selects by detaching them from their wider context. As we have seen, the need to define national identity generally arises when a country's way of life is threatened. Not surprisingly one's definition is shaped by the nature of the threat, and tends to stress only those elements that are under threat. For example, if a community's language or religion is in danger of disappearing or being suppressed, it tends to make them central to its self-conception and subordinates all other constituents of its way of life to them. In short, every definition of national identity is not only partial but also biased and partisan.

This is evident in the way Thatcher defined British national identity. As we have noted, she was deeply worried about the impact of Europe and socialism. Not surprisingly, her fears deeply distorted her definition. By drawing a sharp contrast between Britain and Europe, she misunderstood both. She homogenised Europe, took a highly condescending view of it, and ignored the vast differences between its different countries. So far as Britain was concerned, she completely ignored the European roots of its religious, political, economic and intellectual life, its pre-imperial European entanglements, and the profound influence of European practices and institutions on its development. Her attempt to squeeze out all traces of socialism from the British soul had similar consequences. She suppressed the role of Christian Socialism, the Levellers, the Diggers, the radical and liberal Utilitarians, High Toryism, the "one nation" strand within British thought, and the long and rich tradition of social concern for the under-privileged. Apart from vague references to Elizabeth I, Thatcher rarely looked beyond the 19th century, and even then she never fully understood the latter's deeper structure.[12]

Basically she took a highly moralistic, puritanical and largely petty bourgeois view of British national identity, stressing only those elements that supported the kind of Britain she intended to create. She was determined to rationalise British society, launch the long-delayed capitalist revolution under the petty bourgeois leadership, and to challenge the Establishment in the interests of an upwardly mobile, economically ambitious, socially resentful, morally arrogant and philistine social class. Not surprisingly her view of British national identity assigned no role to the British aristocracy, the trade unions, or to the intellectuals, educationalists, artists and others. It had no room either for British scepticism, humility, self-doubt, sense of irony, deep suspicion of the messiah, spirit of compromise, and healthy respect for divergent views of others. The virtues she stressed were narrowly based, excluded many that the British people have traditionally cherished, and sat ill with each other. Her economic virtues centred around self-interest, and undermined the political virtues that stressed its subordination to the larger interests of the political community. And as for her list of personal virtues, some of them could not be reconciled with her stress on Christianity — as was pointed out by many a religious leader.

Thatcher insisted that Britain was a fundamentally individualist country and that she intended to "set the individual free". Yet she created the most centralised state in British history and violated some of the most essential features of the British way of life. She could not set the individual free without first equipping him with the relevant qualities of temperament and character. And having set him free, she needed to guard against and remedy the inescapable chaos and undesirable consequences that such individuals were bound to create. She had no choice but to turn to the state for both these tasks, especially as she deeply distrusted and destroyed or emasculated almost all the intermediate social and civil institutions. The freed individual necessarily required systematic ordering by a powerful and highly centralised state. This is precisely the criticism she had levelled against the continent of Europe! Far from retrieving and reaffirming British national identity, she in fact subverted it. Ironically she both Europeanised Britain and constructed a political structure ideally suited for socialism. She served her country in a manner almost wholly opposite to what she intended.

One basic lesson of the New Right political discourse is worth emphasising. We must remain deeply suspicious of every attempt to appeal to national identity and to use it to defend a political argument. All statements of national identity are partial and partisan. They reify, homogenise and freeze an inherently complex, internally differentiated and fluid way of life. And they falsely promise to give an ontological foundation to political life. Politics has and can have no other foundation than an inescapably tentative consensus arrived at by free citizens. The consensus can be genuine or manipulated, broadly or narrowly based, grounded in rational discussion or in shallow emotions and prejudices. While we should constantly aim to improve its quality and content, we can never hope to ground it in a non-existent national soul.[13]

## Notes

1. I am grateful to Paul Gilbert, Noël O'Sullivan and Philip Norton for their helpful comments.
2. For a further discussion, see my "Discourses on National Identity" in *Political Studies*, September 1994.
3. For a fuller discussion, see the excellent piece by David Marquand in Robert Skidelsky (ed.), *Thatcherism*, (Oxford: Basil Blackwell, 1989). The Conservative Election Manifesto of 1979 remarked, "Our country's decline is not inevitable. We in the Conservative Party think we can reverse it".
4. Roy Lewis, *Enoch Powell: Principle in Politics* (London: Cassell, 1979), p. 86. See also Enoch Powell, *Joseph Chamberlain* (London: Thames and Hudson, 1977) and *Freedom and Reality* (Kingswood: Elliott Rightway Books, 1969).
5. Ibid, p. 79.
6. Ibid, p. 89.
7. For good discussions of Thatcherism, see Andrew Gamble, *The Free Economy and the Strong State: The Politics of Thatcherism* (London: Macmillan, 1988); Robert Skidelsky, op cit, the articles by Michael Biddiss and S.E. Finer in Kenneth Minogue and Michael Biddiss, (eds) *Thatcherism: Personality and Politics* (London: Macmillan, 1987); and Stuart Hall and Martin Jacques, (eds) *The Politics of Thatcherism* (London: Lawrence and Wishart, 1983).
8. *Newsweek*, April 1992.
9. See her Bruges speech, (London: Conservative Political Centre, 1988), p.1
10. Ibid, p. 2.
11. Ibid, pp. 3f.

12. The partiality of the Thatcherite view of British national identity is striking when contrasted with the following remarks of a distinguished historian.

> "We have a great deal to be ashamed of in our history. We promoted and profited by the slave trade; we plundered India and Africa ... we forced the opium trade on China, attempted to suppress the American, French and Russian Revolutions, and were guilty of centuries of oppression of the Irish people. I do not want a school history which boasts about our victories over lesser breeds — Spaniards, Frenchmen, Germans, Russians, Argentinians — nor over helpless colonial peoples."

Christopher Hill, "History of Patriotism" in Raphael Samuel (ed) *Patriotism: The Making and Unmaking of British National Identity*, Vol. 1, (London: Routledge, 1989).

13. Many in Britain today use the fashionable language of national identity, but often mean nothing more than the kind of society Britain should aim to become. For the Guardian editorials of 8th and 9th May 1990, the "problem of British national identity and ... the possible shape of a new constitutional settlement" are the two important themes of contemporary British politics. "The two themes belong together because the choice of the best type of constitution is inseparable from the settled understanding of who we are. There will be no new constitutional settlement until we resolve that troubled sense of identity". The authors of the editorials then go on to clarify that by identity they mean Britain deciding whether it should be a unitary or a federal state. See also the editorial "The Meaning of Britishness" in the *Times Higher Education Supplement*, May 1993. It rejects the culturally based New Right view of national identity and pleads for a new and open-ended political view "serviceable to today's needs." In these discussions national identity is not given but created, and refers not to the national soul but to clearly developed national goals.

# 8 What is cultural imperialism?

*Paul Gregory*

## Introduction

The word "culture" invites a multitude of meanings. It can be a style of life as typified by a given community or nation. Or it may designate cultural artefacts, namely works of literature, musical compositions, the fine arts and so on. Among such artefacts, the attribution of culture may be reserved for those that are considered profound, complex and therefore serious, as opposed to what is merely entertainment. Or again "culture" may refer to a shared sensibility, as when we speak of a scientific, a religious or a consumer culture.

Now one understanding of "cultural imperialism" is that this is the imposition, by coercion, of "alien" culture in one shape or another. For example, a language might be imposed on a people by forcefully forbidding them the use of their native tongue. There is little to be said philosophically about such cases: a moral defence of such imposition appears inconceivable, and the nature of what is happening seems clear enough. But there are more interesting uses of the expression "cultural imperialism", namely when the victims seem to be willing collaborators in the process.

The "colonised" might consent to "invasion" by a foreign language (and the culture associated with that language) as when, for instance, non-native speakers of English pay (directly or indirectly) for the pleasure of viewing television and other entertainment in English. Or the "colonised" might adopt new eating and drinking habits, which are often less healthy than their traditional ways; easy examples would be the adoption of sweet soft drinks or fast food hamburgers, or else simply of white bread. Pertinent questions here would be how far the change involves the play of prestige, and how far commercial inducements are deployed to wean people from their traditional habits; and then how much the return route has been blocked, as when traditional habits can no longer regain a foothold because the corresponding infrastructure has meanwhile been destroyed.

109

A more intermediate example (between unembellished coercion and willing compliance) would be if, say, a nation is pressurised to license consumer advertising, for instance under threat of trade sanctions. The justification, or rather apology, for such pressure would be that, if a nation wishes to sell its goods it must also be willing to buy those of others, and in a free market the latter may need to have recourse to advertising in order to sell to the citizens of the former.

Those opposed to such "influences", to take a neutral word, might complain of coercion, but the word sits uneasily as long as the influences involved are discreet, indirect and essentially peaceful. More fitting words with which to condemn the "alien" influence would be "corruption" or "seduction". These words are of course pregnant with evaluative connotations, while their factual content is hazy. One task in the following will be to clarify what in matter-of-fact terms may be meant here by corruption and seduction. I shall try to do this by looking at the mechanics by means of which some changes — at various levels of life — get off the ground and impose themselves. Then I shall return to the topic of culture addressed in the opening paragraph and discuss why some culture at least cannot be a commodity. To conclude I shall say something about the effect of market thinking on the general culture.

## Being forced to follow suit

Suppose that, in a world economy governed by the principle of free trade, a change in styles of work is imposed on some nations. It is conceivable,[1] for example, that in order to withstand the trading exploits of the Japanese, which allegedly have their roots in more thorough-going organisation and communication in the workplace, the British one day find it advisable or imperative to adopt the Japanese custom of talking shop when the day's work is finished. Employees would then gather at the company pub and discuss ways of improving procedures on the work floor, the design of the products and the operating manuals, instead of as now going home to their families, their gardens or their videos.

In a similar vein, there have been many instances where over the years, in response to the superior productivity achieved by North American and Western European countries through the rationalization of work routines, other cultures too have been compelled to introduce a radical division of labour with all that such a division of labour means for the lifestyle and work satisfaction of people in (and out of) employment.

There are two issues involved here. One is that such changes to working and leisure practices may involve an intrinsic enrichment or impoverishment, and it is possible to debate which of these is happening, and for which groups within the community, and the extent to which such changes, if they are for the worse, can be compensated for by improved prosperity. A second issue is the mechanics by means of which the changes are instigated.

These mechanics reflect a phenomenon which occurs universally and is encapsulated in phrases such as "forcing others to follow suit" and, less precisely, "forcing the pace".[2] The concept is also embedded in the expressions "competitive armament" and of course "the arms race".

It is the general problem of the conflict of freedoms. In the real world, the exercise by one person or group of their option to do $x$ will very often not prevent others from doing x, but might well instead constrain those others to do $x$, i.e. prevent others from doing *not-x*. In the above example, the people of one nation or culture can unilaterally constrain another or others to a course of action they would not otherwise have chosen. Note that there is here no necessary implication of scheming or wicked intent or the like. It is simply the case that an enormous amount of tacit consensus is required over vast areas of life, ranging from commercial activity on the international scale through to, for example, how fast we drive on a particular stretch of motorway or whether there is piped music at the railway station. As soon as this implicit consensus is broken, and perhaps for the best of reasons, others have little choice but to go along with the change.

## Cultural artefects are not commodities alone

At the GATT talks the Americans tried to stop Europe (and notably France) from protecting and subsidising its film industries in certain ways on the grounds that such protection and subsidies inhibit free trade.[3]

Now it could be argued that the protection involved is justified since the American film industry enjoys certain strategic advantages, most notably its having a huge domestic market, which enable it to keep costs lower than Australian or European producers. This argument is economic in nature and need not detain us further.

Another argument is philosophical in nature. It is that culture is not a commodity. I shall field two arguments as to why cultural artefacts cannot be commodities.

Not everything can be a commodity, since commodities are contingent goods, and not all goods can be contingent: some goods must be good in themselves. This is a logical truth. (Or at least, if it is a truth, then it is a logical truth.) Whether in fact cultural artefacts can be counted among those goods which are not contingent is a separate matter. But since there must be some such goods, there is at least a prima facie case that cultural artefacts may be such goods. And, as such, candidates for exclusion from bargaining over trading rights.

111

A variation on this argument is that not all goods can have exchange value. The notion of exchange, in one shape or another, lies of course at the heart of market doctrine. Like the idea of measurement, as though all things were commensurable.

A market doctrinaire will disclaim ever having said that cultural artefacts, or for that matter a host of other things and services, were commodities alone and no more than that. The doctrine is simply that the economic rewards which sometimes issue from cultural activity are best determined and distributed in accordance with market forces, and that these forces will also spread the costs equitably or, at least, as equitably as any system will.

Yet this "best determined and distributed in accordance with market forces" is itself partly a value judgement and partly a proposition about which system, as a matter of fact, tends to function most reliably or smoothly. The factual claims involved are very probably not sustainable, for reasons that have to do with the inherent difficulty of marketing cultural artefacts and the lack of marketing expertise or orientation among the artistically creative. The value judgement (in favour of a free market for all cultural artefacts) can only be sustained if it is claimed that, whilst indeed some goods cannot be subjected to exchange value thinking, others can, and culture is one of them. Yet if there are any exceptions to exchange value thinking, then culture is surely as a matter of fact one of them. And we have already established that there must, logically, be some such exceptions.

Now the second argument as to why not all cultural artefacts can be commodities.

Cultural artefacts inevitably say something about the society that produces them. Similarly, they are a self-expression of the artist. There is necessarily an intimate link between the cultural artefacts a society produces or uses and the kind of society it is.

In expanding on this train of thought, I will restrict the scope of the argument to consider just one particular group of cultural artefacts, namely those involving narrative. Narrative includes here not only novels, shorter fiction and epic verse, but also most films and even news stories and history.

The narrative a society produces tells us arguably more about its distinctive nature than any number of its other cultural artefacts such as its cuisine, buildings, implements, and musical compositions. Narrative is also linked intimately to language, and may also convey the subtlety and flavour of variations within a language, i.e. dialect, historical tonality, the language of particular professions, characters, etc. Indeed, generally speaking, a culture is identified first and foremost by its language.

The preeminence of narrative can be put differently: A culture reveals itself by the stories it tells. Everybody tells stories, so some stories have to be told. Literature and film merely repeat the procedure on a grander scale.

One of the crucial things narrative and most other art forms do is to hold up a mirror.  Mirrors reflect, and thereby give rise to reflection.

In a manner of speaking, you can't leave others to do your reflecting for you.  Mirrors also provide a nearly identical image; they tell you who, in visual terms, you are.

Mirrors, reflection, identity: — the conclusion of this extended metaphor is that narrative in particular, and perhaps cultural artefacts generally, define a society.    A society without a narrative of its own will therefore also soon lack a cultural identity of its own, becoming inevitably the outpost of another culture.  I think the truth expressed here is a conceptual one, rather than being just a moral platitude that it is desirable for a people to have its own narrative culture.

The practical conclusion that follows from this is that it is imperative for a society or, in a loose sense of the word, a nation to ensure that its own story-tellers, including in our age its film-makers, have the wherewithal to flourish.

Assuming a healthy home-grown narrative culture exists, there is still every reason to seek the stimulus and fertilisation offered by other narrative traditions.  But there will not be any fertilisation if there is no longer a home-grown culture to be fertilised.


## Market culture

Exchange — like its counterfoils, giving and taking — is a fundamental feature of human society.

Markets provide a forum for systematic exchange.  Only the most systematic repression — as in the old Communist countries — has ever succeeded in silencing, for a while, the marketplace.

This said, it is possible to have more or less market.

A distinction can be made between an economy or section of the economy where prices are relatively fixed and uniform, and an economy or sections of an economy where prices are negotiated, i.e. where prices vary constantly in accordance with the laws of supply and demand.  Except in extreme situations, it is possible to pay more or less attention to the negotiation of prices.  You can without undue reflection pay the price that is asked, or accept the price offered, on the assumption that it is the going rate.  Or else *go to the market* to determine whether it is the current rate.

That is, the market serves as a court of appeal, and in a sometimes harsh world the instance of last resort.  The market is a regulatory body, always there in the background if a supplier oversteps the mark or a buyer puts excessive pressure on prices.  It functions in a manner not dissimilar to the law in the case of minor infringements.  Often you can with impunity, say, exceed the speed limit up to a point, which is ill-defined.  Or you tolerate some minor

113

injustice because the onus of proof, the uncertainty and the length of the legal process together make it nonsense to pursue the matter. And so it is that the law of the land just as the law of the marketplace does not apply ineluctably.

One virtue claimed for the market is that, in the long run, it is a better arbiter than planning committees, government decrees, or for that matter regulatory mechanisms. But this claim is an empirical one. There is no guarantee that it will always be the better regulator, or that it is the better regulator in all spheres. Indeed, whereas the empirical evidence from some areas is impressive, it is inconclusive or contradictory in others.

One crucial problem that the market as regulator encounters is that of measurement. How do you assess the performance of doctors and teachers, or novelists and politicians? To be consistent, the market would have to make popularity the crucial test. Yet everyone rejects this criterion.

Arriving at an informed opinion, at an equitable and exact judgement, is often costly if not impracticable. Yet the market of itself cannot deliver its much vaunted benefits without measurement. So, as it becomes more thoroughgoing, market culture leads to a preoccupation with measurement. The ultimate market culture is a culture of measurement: measurement galore to delight the heart of every accountant and bureaucrat in the land!

When pursued to its conclusion, the market idea, far from remaining culturally neutral, becomes itself a key player in the culture of a nation, culture here of course in the sense of a way of life and a sensibility. The worst fate, though, is when a false notion of the market gains currency.

Thus one of the many other virtues claimed for the market is that it turns egoism to the benefit of all. The entrepreneur works for his own material reward, but in so doing profits the whole community. Instead of being interpreted in terms solely of a safety-net function, this individual insight about certain contexts gets vulgarised and is interpreted as a fail-safe mechanism. In place of the claim that a fair dose of egoism can be tolerated, we have the claim, all too palatable to those it pleases, that egoism need never be curbed of itself since the market will see to that; indeed that it is a virtue.[4]

A first failing in this line of thinking is its misplaced trust in the power of market mechanisms. For example, in many cases where the market could in principle have the desired effect in the very long term, it is defeated because players in the market change over the short to medium term (e.g. companies are restructured; or they move away from their original market; or they get new names).

The prevailing dogma fails in the second place because there are areas where the market mechanism has difficulty in even getting a foothold (e.g. for the above-mentioned reasons relating to measurability and the process of marketing).

These two failings are compounded by a third, namely that the argument nurtures a one-sided style of thinking, notably an affirmation of unbridled egoism. This egoism feeds back into cultural structures, i.e. the value system,

114

with the effect that the general culture is mutated and impoverished. Though, it should be said, even without the cultivation of egoism (and indeed envy and status seeking), the ascendency of market thinking cannot be culturally neutral because, as explained, it induces a pervasive preoccupation with measurement.

**Notes**

1.   The examples used throughout are for illustrative purposes only. Most refer to popular conceptions, which may or may not prove to be well founded in fact once examined objectively.

2.   There is a neat German word that says this precisely: *Zugzwang*, which has its original application in the game of chess, as when my opponent forces me to make moves I would prefer to avoid. The word is, interestingly, much loved of political commentators.

3.   What exactly happened is labyrinthine and this description is perhaps misleading. The Americans objected to certain modalities of protection and subsidy. In the background there were other, not uninteresting factors at play. For example, the conflict may be seen as a clash between mass culture and the artistic refinement of an élite. American culture is first and foremost popular culture. Another factor is the acceptability among European audiences of dubbing in contrast to American sensibilities in this respect.

4.   Robert C. Solomon prefaces his superb book "Ethics and Excellence" (Oxford University Press, 1992) with a quotation from *Hamlet* (III, iv), which is apposite here too:

> For in the fatness of these pursy times,
> Virtue itself of vice must pardon beg.

# 9 Communities of obligation

*David Gosling*

## Introduction

This paper explores some aspects of the relationship between political change and philosophical theory, namely the connections between the creation of an ideology of "Europeaness" and "partialism" in ethics. Recent defences of partialist ethics seem to provide an apology for a narrowing of ethical obligations which, in the context of the current redefinition of the European "community" as a political and economic unit, has potentially serious implications for those who fall outside the defined boundaries of "European-ness". To challenge this theoretical justification of Eurocentrism, it is necessary to question the assumptions underpinning both the new "community" of Europe and also the growing popularity of ethical partialism.

The rhetoric proclaims the new Europe as an experiment in internationality, but the political reality is that a more narrow Eurocentric perspective is being given a renewed economic strength and a new political structure. As a result of the new institutions of Europe, special "associative" obligations within the "Community" will predictably become more demanding as interdependence and closer cooperation become more common. Given the presumption that a community's first loyalties and duties are to those who are its internal members, aid will increasingly be directed towards populations regarded as deprived within the Community, while aid to developing nations, where needs are much greater, will be discretionary because they are defined as external to Europe.

Policies on asylum and immigration, as well as aid policies, are already showing evidence of becoming more discriminatory because the newly defined Europe is, I shall argue, based on a presumed shared ethnicity. Specific obligations which may be thought to arise from the colonial past[1] are being increasingly ignored because of the claims of internal priorities. While there is every likelihood that the European Community will continue to be a source of aid to underdeveloped countries, the possibility of any radical reassessment

117

of the terms of trade between major economic powers and the poorest nations in the world may be made more difficult by the new political groupings within a common Europe.

Applied philosophy should have something to say about these matters which are of practical and immediate political concern as they affect (1) political and economic relations with under-developed countries, (2) individuals from these countries seeking entry into Europe and (3) those already here who suffer a variety of types of discrimination against them both in official policies and through everyday acts of racism. Clearly it is not possible in the context of a philosophical paper to consider all the matters which are relevant to the creation of the conditions in which racism can flourish. But by identifying the assumptions implicit in the discourse of the new Europe about our moral obligations and subjecting them to analysis and criticism, applied philosophy can make an important contribution.

## The ideology of "Europeaness"

A view about what has been happening in Europe's recent history has been eloquently expressed by the historian J. G. A. Pocock, who argues that the formation of the European Community has been accompanied by an ideology of "Europeaness" which has:

> "affirmed that the culture possessed in common by these national communities, and the history of this common culture, was of greater moral and ideological significance than their several distinct national sovereignties or than the history shaped and written — as the classical age of European historiography had been written — by their several histories."[2] However, Pocock goes on to say, "Europe" continues to mean different things to different people, for two reasons. Firstly because it is geographically undefined — "the frontiers of Europe" towards the east are everywhere open and indeterminate" — and secondly because the "ideology of Europeaness", which has "enjoined the rejection of previously distinct national identities without proposing a synthetic or universal history to take their place", has met with only limited acceptance. As a result the processes of change through which we are living involve a counterpoint between "the homogenisation of cultures" and "the maintenance in the present of identity as members of coherent communities possessing coherent and recollectable pasts."[3]

Writing as someone whose origins were in New Zealand, Pocock reflects that national communities who had previously regarded themselves as part of

118

"British" culture have had to redefine their identity in non-European terms, because of the specific changes in British policy. "Europe", he suggests, may find that it has the power to determine when a community is or is not "European", but "not the authority to command the consent of the cultures affected, which can alone legitimate the inclusion or exclusion of empire".

This restructuring of identities occurs at an individual as well as at a political and economic level. Individual citizens are changing their identities, whether they wish to or not, because the political communities of which they are members and which define in part their personal identity are changing. We may approach this question of how redefinition occurs at two levels, which reflect two historiographical traditions. According to one view, a person's historical identity is a given, part of one's social reality, embedded in language, social practices and customs. We are forced to recognise this common identity sometimes *despite* ourselves, when we discover an affinity with someone from a similar background, when we find ourselves being nostalgic for particular artefacts, ways of dressing, pieces of music, gestures, turns of speech with which we identify. We may react with fondness or antipathy to the recognition of our cultural identity, but either way we cannot deny it; its objective reality cannot be gainsaid.

But on another view all history, including our sense of ourselves as inheritors of a history, is a construction, an amalgam and "hybridisation", the result of a selection from a multiplicity of possibilities. What we take at any given time to be objective reality turns out, on this view, to derive from both personal choices and socially defined meanings. How this selection occurs requires careful analysis of a multitude of cultural, political and economic influences, most of which are not directly apparent to the individuals who are subject to them, although individual choices do collectively create significant trends which shape the culture. These choices are, however, made within frameworks which are often largely determined by political and economic elites.

This bifurcation between "reality" and "construction" is misleading. At the phenomenological level, the individual's experience of social reality appears to be given, but cultural analysis reveals the ways in which the transformation of experience is influenced and selected. Social meanings do not come to us in fixed categories, rather we have to construct an identity by reference to different elements, each of which inflects the other. From a range of possibilities we "articulate" an identity by combining elements which contribute to our sense of ourselves. The process of "articulation" is not simply the summing of discrete elements. As Jonathan Rutherford has put it:

> Identity is constituted out of different elements of experience and subjective position, but in their articulation they become something more than just the sum of their original elements. For example our class subjectivities do not simply co-exist alongside

119

our gender. Rather our class is gendered and our gender is classed. Making our identities can only be understood within the context of this articulation, in the intersection of our everyday lives with the economic and political relations of subordination and domination.[4]

Cultural diversity, the proliferation of possible identities and the failure of the religious and ethical traditions of the West to maintain their hold over the imaginations of the populace mean that this process of articulation has become more complex, less stable and therefore more open to manipulation. Histories can be rewritten and languages can be given new vocabularies, and this is precisely what Pocock is suggesting is happening in creating the "ideology of Europeaness".

Much the same process, it might be said, has occurred in the creation of national identities. As a number of writers have pointed out, the sense of nationality is created over time through a variety of processes of mythologising and symbolisation to create what Benedict Anderson calls "imagined communities".[5] As such, national identities, and the perception of loyalties which attach themselves to nationhood, are creations, often of political elites who have consolidated their power through bureaucratic incorporation of previously disparate communities. But, as Smith as argued, "ethnic" elements of common myths of origin and descent, common memories and common symbols are interpenetrated with political, territorial, educational and economic elements which may be termed "civic" in the creation of the modern nation.[6]

The creation of the supra-national unit, the European *Economic* Community, has been primarily driven by economic considerations, rather than because of an enlightened desire to create a community. The willingness to accept the partial dissolution of the nation state is the result of changing perceptions about what it is in the interest of the individual member states to accept. It is primarily driven by a concern to improve economic opportunities and to provide a defensive economic union to withstand the power of the Japanese economy and newly industrialised states. The primary motivation has been the belief that there is no alternative economic network which could serve the same function with the same effect and therefore the main players in the formation of the new Europe have "no alternative" but to be inside the community rather than be left as outsiders.

The achievement of the economic goal requires that previously separate and distinct nations, who in recent history were on opposite sides in the Second World War, undertake the process of bureaucratic incorporation into a supra-state. But this is not sufficient to create a stable political unity — it is also necessary, in Smith's words, to appeal to "common myths, memories and symbols to create and preserve networks of solidarity that underpin and characterise nations".[7] The importance of these shared categories of meanings is that they are essential to make sense of political groupings and create new individual and social identities. David Miller has argued that, "it is constitutive of national identity that members of a nation have characteristics in common which make it appropriate for them to be lumped together politically, rather than parcelled out in some other way."[7] The almost arbitrary boundaries of the "European Community" make it especially important to attempt to construct a common identity.

But where does this leave the cultural diversity which is so much a characteristic of modern western states? Miller suggests a distinction between a "relatively thin" kind of common public culture, and a "private" culture where a plurality of subcultures can coexist. However, in the context of the socialist ideals he is defending, he argues:

> Subcultures threaten to undermine the overarching sense of identity that socialists are looking for. They are liable to do so in two ways: they give participants a narrower focus of loyalty that may pre-empt commitments to the wider community; and by way of reaction people outside a particular subculture may find it difficult to identify with those seen in some way separated off.[8]

In order to protect the people's commitment to the nation state within a multicultural society, Miller is prepared to argue that the history taught in schools should be selective in its account of the nation's past in order to help make it possible for members of the minority subculture to feel at home in and loyal to the state.[9] If the creation of an ideology of Europeaness is successful, a version of history will one day need to be taught in schools across the whole "Community" which fulfils this same role of enabling all its members to feel loyalty to the supra-state.

However, I wish to argue that the search for an overarching social identity is misguided. Whether as a dominant identity within a nation state or within an "ideology of Europeaness", this notion is not only a threat to the manner in which many citizens within a pluralist state, or within the still more pluralist Europe, can *belong*, but also one that is likely to have a deleterious influence on Europe's perception of its position on wider global issues. The problem arises because of the manner in which identity is seen as being relative to a dominant culture. Miller treats cultural pluralism as a private matter, as if it were distinct from the public domain of the state and can therefore be "tolerated". Difference is allowed by the dominant group only as long as it poses no threat to the dominant culture. This is an attempt to place limits on the forms of articulation that can be tolerated within a political community and, as such, it clearly works against certain groups being accepted on the same terms as those whose articulated identity is regarded as less problematic.

The impact of these and similar ideas can be seen in the current developments in the political discourse of Europe. Because constructing a sense of community is believed to require a common feature, the "ideology of European-ness" must necessarily appeal to the only characteristic that Europeans have in common, namely their European-ness. By talking about common origins and shared histories and in constructing a discourse of the "same", boundaries must be drawn against imagined "others". Because Europeaness is the primary signifier of "sameness", an implicitly racist discourse is created which builds upon a deep-seated network of beliefs about racial superiority which underpin European's sense of their common identity. This sense of Europe's "destiny" as the centre of civilisation, as the reference point for high culture, has its roots in Hegelian notions of progress and Darwinian evolution; it is arguably the focal point around which the Eurocentric "episteme" is constructed.

If this thesis is correct it explains the implicit assumption that ethnically non-European minorities are problematic in a way that ethnic Europeans are not. It also forges a conceptual link between the political and legal moves to tighten border controls, increase internal surveillance, use social security benefits as a means of checking the legality of visible minorities, and indeed the illegal and violent activities of racist youth groups who have attacked immigrants, desecrated graves, and plundered mosques and synagogues. At the fringes of Europe's official political parties of the right are unofficial groups whose activities are either condoned as "understandable" or actively supported by "respectable" politicians.

The consequences are that peoples of North African descent in France, and people of Afro-Caribbean or Asian descent in Britain become obvious targets, because ethnic difference is believed to be clear in every sense. But what is to count as ethnically European becomes increasingly arbitrary the further Europe spreads eastwards. The problem Europe faces, because of the manner in which it has defined itself, is that either it makes decisions about exclusion entirely in terms of the self-interest of the existing members of the community or else it is based on loose geographical and ethnic criteria and therefore becomes too large to succeed in the political ends which some member states have looked forward to. Refugees from the Yugoslavian conflict, particularly when they are Muslims from Bosnia, Albanian refugees, Turks and Kurds and possible future refugees from many other potential conflicts in the southern states of the old Soviet Union will find themselves scrutinised to determine how far they are acceptable to an ethnic conception of Europeaness.

Political change of this kind does not happen smoothly. Conflicts and contradictions remain. The drive to create an overarching identity or community of shared interests at a European level and the attempts to create or revive a common sense of "being European" is largely, I have argued, a post-facto construction in order to ease the path of various harmonisation programmes required to ease the flow of market goods. But with harmonisation there also comes resistance, for the "political sentiment", which nation-states have engendered to create "imagined communities", does not yet exist in much

122

of the new Europe. The economic self-interest of states is not powerful enough to dissolve the alternative features which tie peoples together — in particular language, shared customs, religion and culture — into more local loyalties. The result is that at the local level citizens resent the Brussels bureaucracy and continue to see it as alien. Far from the European Community being perceived as encompassing and inclusive of its member states it remains in the imagination as external.

Yet, despite this resistance to the Brussels bureaucracy, there are disturbing signs that the need to feel a common identity as "Europeans" is producing the rise in racism which this analysis suggests is entailed by the manner in which European identity is being constructed. In Germany a new phrase is "international nationalism" — meaning the common interests of people from European "stock" against the groups of immigrants and asylum seekers who, though different in their ethnic origin in the various European states, are all nevertheless grouped together as the "others" who threaten the European ideal. Although much of the thinking behind the nationalist movements in Europe is confused and philosophically unsophisticated, I want now to see how far a philosophical trend towards partialism may offer support to these political trends.

## Partialism

How does the restructuring of communities' identities in the process of creating the new Europe have any effect on our moral obligations? The relevance of identity to moral thinking is asserted by a certain view about how moral obligations arise, namely what has been defended as "partialist" or "particularist" ethics. For what lies behind the difficulties I have been alluding to is a view which is widely shared and which has recently been defended in the philosophical literature; namely that it is morally right to prioritise duties to individuals and groups who may in some sense be thought of as our own. It has been asserted that, in order to avoid the "fantasy ethics"[11] of global impartiality, it is necessary to recognise that moral agents owe their primary duties to those closest to them in terms of kinship, friendship and locality. Personal fulfilment requires that we have relationships of trust and affection with particular individuals and groups to whom we are bound by ties of loyalty. According to this view, personal integrity only has meaning in the context of these close relationships which determine our values and establish our duties. Such duties arising from closeness of kinship take priority over other possible actions which a purely impartial calculation of good-maximisation might suggest. This is not simply a matter of psychological or practical observation, that, as a matter of fact, "All of us accord massive priority to our own plans and projects, families, loved ones, friends",[12] for it is specifically a moral claim that it is *morally correct* to prioritise one's own personal commitments.

Those who make such claims often attempt to substantiate them by reference to our shared intuitions about what we would consider right in specific circumstances — such as whether to save one's own daughter or someone else's from drowning or from a burning building. To fail to save one's own on the grounds of impartiality would open one to the accusation of being, on one account, "a great fool, an object of pity and contempt" and on another "an object of moral contempt, a moral leper".[13] Certainly it is difficult to disagree about such examples (even if one wanted to), but I wonder how much is actually established by these cases and how much they help us once we move away from life-and-death issues within one's own family (though even here I suspect there are unexamined cultural assumptions at work). Should loyalty require a father to defend his daughter against accusations of bullying when there is substantial evidence to support her guilt and when the victim of the bullying has committed suicide? However, even if we think it is somehow natural for a father or mother to defend their child, the intuitive approval for such a view becomes less certain as soon as we move from the closest circles of preference to wider groups of one's community, country, religious or racial group. An unqualified partialism, in Cottingham's own words, and speaking as someone who has defended this view, "appears to licence chauvinist and racist behaviour of the kind that most serious moral thinkers would unreservedly condemn".[14]

Before I address this issue I would like to make some links to my earlier discussion of identities. It is sometimes made to appear in the literature on partialism that the historical and affective affinities which determine our sense of obligation are relatively fixed, unchosen and in a sense "inevitable".[15] MacIntyre, for example, argues that

> I inherit from the past of my family, my city, my tribe, my nation, a variety of debts, inheritances, rightful expectations and obligations. These constitute the given of my life, my moral starting point. This is in part what gives my life its own moral particularity.....For the story of my life is always embedded in the story of those communities from which I derive my identity.[16]

But I have argued that social identity is articulated relative to a variety of communities that a person finds him or herself a member of — the communities of class, gender, sexual preference, religious group, ethnic origin, political affiliation and so on. What is regarded as significant depends on how these social groups are represented within the communicative practices and discourses of the group to which a person aligns him or herself. The "debts, inheritances, rightful expectations and obligations" of which MacIntyre speaks do not emerge unproblematically and uncontentiously from the historicised self.

124

There are a multiplicity of possible and conflicting obligations which can be derived from "those communities from which I derive my identity."

Similarly when Oldenquist argues that "patriotic considerations are, for people who have a basis for patriotism, genuinely normative considerations, partly determinative of what they should do, all things considered,"[17] he fails to take account of the extent to which individual citizens may stand in different relationships to the nation. The multiplicity of different personal histories will create many possible perceptions of what is due to the state. Patriotism cannot be required equally of all, nor can any specific duty be required of all in the name of patriotism.

Different interpretations of history produce different perceptions of obligations. An example concerns the relationship of Europe with its ex-colonial territories.

On one view the most important commonality is that between the colonising powers who shared the experience of entering and ruling the undeveloped nations, bringing Christianity, civilisation and trade. But an alternative view, which was until recently celebrated by the colonial powers themselves, emphasised the common bond between the colonial power and the former colonies. On this view the countries within greater France, which included the colonies, had more in common, culturally and institutionally, than France had with, say, Britain and its "Commonwealth", differing as it does in language, parliamentary tradition, educational system and much else. This alternative history, which links each colonial power with its former colonies, has the potential to identify obligations to immigrant communities from those states and, arguably, some duties to continue favourable trading relations to compensate for the exploitation of those states while recognising their right to self-determination. By choosing to identify with the other European colonial powers the European Community is perpetuating neo-colonialism without any significant commitment to substantially alter the relationship between the metropolitan centre and the under-developed ex-colonies.

By rejecting the shared history between coloniser and colonised in favour of a shared history between colonisers, the commonality within the construct "European" is being prioritised over previously favoured constructs. Thus ethnic identity is preferred over ethnic plurality. Because partialism appears to justify this choice, it is legitimate to raise the doubt that Cottingham himself identifies, namely that partialism appears to justify racism and chauvinism.

The partialist has two options about how to reply here. One is to show that moral preferences based on social groupings are defensible and right; the other is to show that it is possible to provide a basis for distinguishing a morally defensible form of the thesis from that which leads to "chauvinist and racist" conclusions. It is not only ethnic groupings that are relevant here — consider also partiality based on religion, gender, sexual preference, class, political affiliation, or even academic subject ("We philosophers should stick together").

Cottingham adopts the position that "in the case of racial partiality there appears to be no remotely plausible case for arguing that it must find a place in all or most plausible blueprints for human welfare" and argues that this is supported by "empirical evidence".[18] But without qualification this does not appear to be the case. When a racial group is in a minority and oppressed by some larger, more powerful racial group, it would appear to be both morally defensible and empirically more likely to contribute to the welfare of those concerned for them to give preference to members of their own racial group. The empirical evidence on whether one's welfare is better promoted by giving partiality to members of one's own ethnic group is surely too inconclusive and too open to alternative interpretations for us to be confident, on the basis of evidence alone, that morally abhorrent forms of racism will be eliminated. Partiality within ethnic groups is as defensible as any other form of partialism when it contributes to a person's sense of self-worth, enables them to pursue a chosen life-plan and to form fulfilling relationships. When loyalty to one's own people constitutes a framework within which a meaningful self-identity can be maintained, then it is difficult to condemn it outright as unethical.

But the justifiable benefits of partialism must be qualified, and these qualifications are essential if partialism is not to appear to give support to racist ideologies. The first qualification is the need for recognition that overwhelming need calls for a sufficient response by those who have the appropriate knowledge and the capacity to act. Unless this qualification is recognised, partialism is indistinguishable from group self-interest. If I have been right to suggest that the primary motivation for the European Community has been to protect the economic self-interest of some of the richest states on the globe, then it is a legitimate concern that the subsequent redrawing of the limits of obligation to within the boundaries of Europe will have the consequence of ignoring greater levels of need and the problems of global inequality and poverty. The ethics of partialism always runs the risk of failing to meet the demands of the greatest needs if these happen to fall outside the boundaries of the communities to which we owe our immediate loyalties. The combination of self-interested political activity and a partialist ethic must be open to this criticism — that unconditional duty to alleviate the greatest levels of need is eclipsed by the more immediate demands made by those within the boundaries of the community of political allegiances.

Secondly, partialism must be qualified by limitations which prevent the benefits of giving priority to one's own accruing at the expense of exploiting others or suppressing the opportunities for other groups to adopt their own group identities and pursue their own goals. The only defensible form of partialism is one supplemented by an impartial commitment to other ethical standards, namely those of tolerance of cultural heterogeneity, of equality of opportunity and participation in social and political life, and of respect for and response to individual human needs. This is in part because, as I have argued,

126

social identity is not a given, but is, rather, always open to re-definition. By recognising that our own identity is not a fixed category, we can appreciate the possibility of ways in which we may share identity with others who appear different. Whatever loyalties we have to our "own", we must accept the rights of "others" to form relationships within groups which are equally entitled to participate in society. These rights override partial considerations, and, for this reason, the morality of partiality must be qualified by universal standards if it is not to become an apology for racism and chauvinism.

## Bibliography

Anderson, B. *Imagined Communities: Reflections on the Origin and Spread of Nationalism*, Verso, 1983

Cottingham, J. "Partiality, Favouritism and Morality" in *The Philosophical Quarterly*, Vol 36, No. 144, 1986

Gellner, E. *Nations and Nationalism*, CUP, 1983

Gosling, D. W. "Obligations of the Affluent nations to the Poor" in Twining, W. (ed.): *Issues of Self-Determination* Aberdeen University Press, 1991

MacIntyre, A. *After Virtue*, Duckworth, 1980

Mackie, J. *Ethics: Inventing Right and Wrong*, Harmondsworth, 1977

Miller, D. *Market, State and Community: Theoretical Foundations of Market Socialism*, Clarendon, 1989

Pettit, P. "Social Holism and Moral Theory," *Aristotleian Society Proceedings*, 1985-86, pp 173-197

Oldenquist, A. "Loyalties" in *The Journal Of Philosophy*, Vol LXXIX, No. 4, April 1982

Pocock, J.G.A. *Deconstructing Europe*, London Review of Books, Vol 13, No. 24, 19 Dec 1991

Ree, J. Internationality, *Radical Philosophy*, Spring 1992

Rutherford, J. (ed.) *Identity, Community, Culture, Difference*, Lawrence & Wishart, 1990

Smith, A. D. *The Ethnic Origin of Nations*, Blackwell, 1986

Smith, A. D. "The Origins of Nations" in *Ethnic and Racial Studies*, Vol 12, No. 13, No. 3, July 1989

## Bibliographical References

1. Gosling, D. W., 1991, p. 58-66
2. Pocock, 1991, p. 6
3. Ibid, p. 8
4. Rutherford, 1990, p. 19
5. Anderson, 1983
6. Smith, 1986, 1989
7. Smith, 1989, 349-50
8. Miller, 1989, p. 244
9. Ibid, p. 279
10. Ibid, p. 291
11. See Mackie, 1977, p. 129 ff
12. Cottingham, 1986, p. 357
13. Oldenquist, 1982, p. 186; Cottingham, 1986, p. 357
14. Cottingham, 1986, p. 359.
15. Pettit, 1986, p. 187
16. MacIntyre A., 1980, p. 205
17. Oldenquist, 1982, p. 187
18. Cottingham, 1986, p. 371

# 10 The dynamics of alignment and antagonism between the societal institutions of market, state and culture

*Gordon Burt*

## 1. Introduction

Contemporary developments in Europe are marked by intense ferment surrounding the social institutions of market, state and culture. According to some the collapse of communist rule in the Soviet Union and Eastern Europe, together with the rolling back of the state in the West, marked the final triumph of the market over the state — one writer even proclaimed the end of history. However, the rise of the market is not universally or unreservedly welcomed. The church expresses concern about a spiritual void, with the Pope warning that the replacement of the state by the market in Eastern Europe needs to be constrained by the culture of Christianity. Nationalism too is in the ascendant as the fears expressed by President Gorbachev in 1988 come to pass: that the collapse of the Soviet state (and we might add the other communist states in Eastern Europe) would bring about the rise of nationalism and conflict between ethnic groups. In this way market, state and culture are in ferment.

This ferment prompts us to look back over the history of relations between the institutions of market, state and culture. The balance between these institutions changes over time. The dominance of the state in Eastern Europe appeared to all but extinguish the existence of market, nation and religion. Yet now the state is weakened and market, religion and nation are burgeoning. In the West too the "post-war consensus" granted the state a pivotal position. Here also the arrangement went into crisis and state power receded somewhat as market forces were given greater rein. Yet this "achievement" is itself under threat, so anti-federalists in the UK argue, from the "Bonapartist" statism of the EC. It is this phenomenon of the shifting balance of power between the key social institutions which forms one of the two central themes of this paper.

The second central theme concerns relations between institutions and actors. For contemporary European history has been marked by popular displays, sometimes of allegiance, sometimes of challenge, to institutions: in the East the throng which greeted the Pope's visit to Poland; the exodus from East Germany; the celebrations on top of the Berlin Wall; the demonstrations in Moscow against the attempted coup of 1991; and in the West, albeit of a different nature, the poll tax protests in the UK; the strikes in Germany; and the rioting in Los Angeles. Here too we can note fluctuations — between quiescence and activism, between allegiance and challenge. This reflects a shifting balance of power.

It is the purpose of this paper to develop a general model of society which allows us to consider these two themes. In section 2 we focus on the shifting balance of power between the institutions themselves and then switch our attention to look at the shifting balance of power between institutions and actors in section 3.

## 2. The balance of power between institutions

### 2.1 The institutional power trajectory

In this section we tackle the first of our themes: the modelling of the shifting balance of power between key social institutions. The introduction cited key figures such as the Pope and President Gorbachev — as well as the anti-federalists in the UK — offering their own analysis of the changing scene. We start our model-building by identifying the basic ingredients of their analyses.

The first point to note is that the cases concern key institutions in society: state, nation, market, religion and culture. Secondly attention is directed to the distribution of power between these institutions. Next changes in this distribution of power are noted. Values are expressed concerning these changes. Finally action is urged to ensure that changes are in a desirable direction.

I shall now express these characteristics in geometrical terms. Consider a *power space* with three dimensions representing the powers of state, nation and market respectively. Where society is at any point in time can be represented by a point in this space. Societal change is represented by a line in this space — a *power trajectory*.

Let us assume that society is normally constrained to move within a particular region — possibly a surface — of power space. One can refer to this as the *feasible power surface*. The power trajectory then lies on this surface.

Let us now apply this model to the anti-federalist argument. The anti-federalists argue that the European state will increase in power causing a decline in the power of the market and of national culture. Their argument can be represented as positing the power trajectory depicted in Diagram 2.1.1.

Diagram 2.1.1 **The power trajectory of rising Eurostate power**

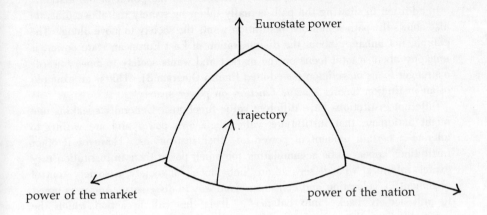

Diagram 2.1.2 **The power trajectory of disintegrating East European state power**

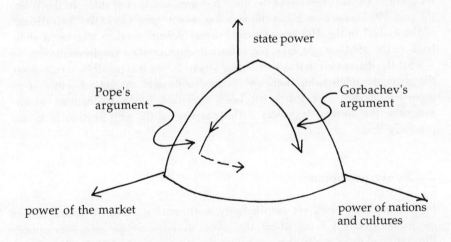

Gorbachev's argument can also be represented as a trajectory: the decline of state power and the rise of national power. See Diagram 2.1.2. The diagram also shows the trajectory corresponding to the Pope's argument that the decline of state power is being accompanied by the rise of the power of the market.

In addition to showing the path actually taken by society the above diagram also shows the path which one institution wants the society to move along. The church, not unhappy about the disintegration of East European state power, is unhappy about a total focus on the market and wants society to move towards a stronger focus on religion (see dotted line in Diagram 3). This is an example of an institution having a *value function* on power space.

Different institutions have different value functions. Generally speaking one might anticipate that institutions value their own power and are willing to tolerate a certain amount of power for other institutions. However if other institutions appear to be accumulating too much power then an institution may express alarm at what it sees as an "imbalance" of society, a society "out of alignment". Toleration and consensus give way to dissensus. Action is urged to pull society back "into balance". It is this call to action which the anti-federalists, President Gorbachev and the Pope were voicing. (Notice that notions of balance and alignment are conditional on the value function; out of quotes I use the balance of power to refer to the distribution of power).

Shifting our attention to a longer span in time we may observe not a unidirectional movement but a trajectory characterised by fluctuation in the balance of power. The relation between church and state in Russia over the century illustrates this, with the contemporary situation pointing to a return in the direction of the balance which existed around the turn of the century — a return after the suppression of the church during communist rule. In the West the post 1945 consensus about the mixed economy gave way to the "privatising of the globe" in the 1980s and some current debate wonders whether a shift back in the 1990s might take place towards greater state involvement.

What the discussion in this section has shown is that it is possible to represent the dynamic relationship between culture state and market in terms of a geometric model. What has not been modelled is the mechanism which generates the societal trajectory. The purpose of the next section is to do precisely that.

## 2.2 Power positioning

In this section I shall set out in fairly mathematical terms a model of the mechanisms which bring about the power trajectory. To give some prior illustration of these mechanisms consider the arguments which have taken place in the UK regarding the European Community. As has been noted, the strength of the EC is feared because it is thought to lead to a diminution of the power of nation and market. While this fear has led some to argue an isolationist position, the argument which has tended to prevail has been the argument for "realism": despite the disadvantages of the EC, it is going to grow in importance and power — whether we like it or not. If we stay out we shall be powerless and unable to influence its decisions which may be against our interests. Far better therefore to play a full part — for this will give us the power which will enable us to moderate their decisions. In this way the power positioning of the UK influences the trajectory of the EC. The model which we are about to develop is intended to capture the essential features of this process.

(i) Agents
First we consider the agents: the two *institutions*, state s and market m.

(ii) Situation
Next we consider the current situation.
Each institution has a certain amount of *power*: $\pi(s)$ , $\pi(m)$.
This allows us to consider a two-dimensional *power space*.
So the *societal position* in power space is given by the point $[\ \pi(s)\ ,\ \pi(m)\ ]$.
Also each institution occupies a *role position* in *role space*.

(iii) Action space
Next we consider the possible actions. Consider the *action space* of all possible actions, { a(i) }. Societal action is the combined action of the institutions — thus *societal action space* consists of multiple copies of action space, { a(i,j) }.

Action involves the use of power to effect change, the exercise of power having a certain "productivity". Here we represent action in terms of exerting power in an attempt to change the distribution of institutional power in a certain direction.

However, different role positions are more productive than others for making the desired change. So there is a two-stage action here: role positioning followed by pressure for change.

(iv) Objective possibility space
The complete situation determines the action which takes place (up to random variation). Taking just part of the situation as given, these given aspects form a constraint on what actions are possible — this gives a possibility space given these situational aspects. The action which eventually occurs must lie within this space.

Commonly the physical features of the situation are taken as given, leaving the ideational features to determine which of the actions in physical possibility space will actually occur.

The objective possibility space is not identical with subjective possibility space. The subjective space suffers errors of omission and of commission.

133

E.g. most subjective scenarios constructed in the mid 1980s would not have envisaged the subsequent actions which took place in Eastern Europe.

## (v) Meaning systems and processes

Subjective possibility space is just as important as objective possibility space. In general, systems of meaning are central to what happens in society. Unfortunately this point is undeveloped in the present paper. However a few observations are worth making. The criteria which we are about to discuss and which we portray as the ideational driving force for action are simply the tip of the iceberg. They are simply the ideational contact points with action. Underlying these criteria are rich systems of meaning and rich meaning processes.

The people of Eastern and Western Europe have lived inside quite different systems of meaning. People inside the church or inside a nation live inside quite different systems of meaning from those who live outside the church, or outside the nation.

## (vi) Criteria

We now consider the criteria for action. This involves values and power.

Each institution attaches a certain *value* to each position x in power space: $v(x,s)$ ; $v(x,m)$. Thus each institution has a *value function*.

We recall that there is a two-stage action here: role positioning followed by pressure for change. Role positioning is important in the following way. Different role positions empower differentially. Secondly different role positions constrain their occupants to different action positions.

Role positions can be located in the actor-power space. Power accruing to the role can thus be represented by an *empowerment function* which grants power to different positions, $em\pi(x, X)$; it depends on the position concerned, x, and the societal position, $X(t)$. The position in actor-power space can also be taken as the action position for the actor.

In determining where it should position itself each institution takes into account both the value it places on that position and the power which that position will generate for itself. The resultant worth of each position will involve a trade-off between value and empowerment. Each institution has a *worth trade-off function* which establishes this trade-off:

$$w(s) = w((v,em\pi),s)w(m) = w((v,em\pi),m)$$

This trade-off function enables us to define a *worth function* which indicates the consequent worth of each position: $w(x,s)$ ; $w(x,m)$.

## (vii) Action

The criteria are applied to determine the action.

Each institution takes up a position which *maximises worth*.

$$x(s) = \{ \ x : w((v(x),\pi(x,X)),s) \text{ is a maximum } \}$$

$$x(m) = \{ \ x : w((v(x),\pi(x,X)),m) \text{ is a maximum } \}$$

(viii) Consequences

The consequences of the action are deduced.

These positions yield the corresponding worth outcomes, value satisfactions and powers to each institution.

However, the institutional positions combine to form the societal position. This is the resultant combination of the two positions weighted by their relative empowerment.

$$X(t+1) = em\pi(s)x(s) + em\pi(m)s(m)$$

In this way the dynamic interaction between the two institutions determines where society is, where the two institutions are, the empowerment they receive, the worth outcomes they obtain and the value satisfactions they gain (i.e. $X,x,\pi,w,v$).

What about the functions themselves — the value function, the empowerment function and the worth function? These might be taken as fixed. Alternatively it seems reasonable to suggest that they are moulded by what happens in society. Notably recent debate surrounding the Labour Party in the UK has posited both changes in values and changes in the trade-off between values and power. Interestingly the debate partly addressed the question of whether values had really changed or simply that a different trade-off was being made.

Perhaps the simplest way of moderating the value function is by introducing a weighting of the worth function. In this way values are partly shaped by contemporary "realities" — values become aligned with what has power.

$$v((x,s),t+1) = z \ v((x,s),t) + z' \ w((x,s),t)$$

The trade-off between power and values may also change. The relative weightings of these in the worth trade-off are likely to be shifted according as a values stance is successful or unsuccessful.

Let us return now to the illustration discussed at the start of this section. The argument between the anti-federalists and the government was between idealists and pragmatists — i.e. between different trade-offs between power and value. The substance of the argument by the government focused on the fact that we would have more power if we placed ourselves inside the EC — i.e. they drew attention to the empowerment function. By such positioning they were thus able to exercise greater power over the future trajectory of the EC — to pull the trajectory of the EC in a direction which grants more power to the nation and the market. In this way the balance of power between the institutions of market, state and nation is formed.

135

## 2.3 The geometry of the model

The model has been developed algebraically. This algebra can be illustrated geometrically. As we do this I shall take the opportunity of making some additional observations regarding the key concepts.

Section 2.1 has already provided the geometrical illustration of societal history as a trajectory of points in power space. Of particular interest at any point in time is the power structure and the potential dominance of one particular institution.

Diagram 2.3.1 illustrates a possible value function for the market institution. Value functions may reflect pure self-interest or some degree of interdependence — possibly even being egalitarian and having a symmetric form (cf. Rawls' concept of justice). Alternatively value functions may be contingent (cf. the final equation of the previous section) — possibly reflecting the conservatism of "where we're at".

Diagram 2.3.2 illustrates the empowerment function. Empowerment is likely to be greatest at the centre of society — where society is at. Empowerment falls off more rapidly with decreasing power levels than with increasing power levels, and differentially for changes in dominant versus non-dominant powers.

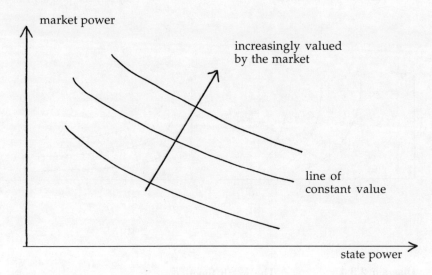

**Diagram 2.3.1** Value function for the market institution

market power

increasingly valued
by the market

line of
constant value

state power

**Diagram 2.3.2** The empowerment function

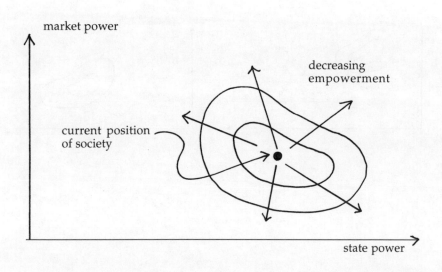

market power

decreasing
empowerment

current position
of society

state power

137

Diagram 2.3.3      The worth trade-off .....

(a) ..... for idealists                              (b) ..... for pragmatists

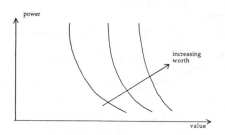
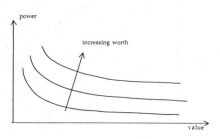

Diagram 2.3.4                The worth function .....

(a) ..... for idealists                              (b) ..... for pragmatists

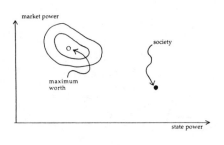
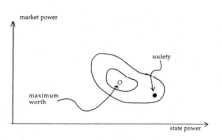

Diagrams 2.3.3 (a) and (b) illustrate the worth trade-off for an idealist and a pragmatist respectively. The idealist weights value much more strongly than empowerment.

Diagrams 2.3.4 (a) and (b) illustrate the consequent worth functions. The idealist gives maximum worth to a position which is more distant from the position of maximum empowerment and which has greater value.

Diagram 2.3.5 illustrates the determination of the societal position as the resultant of the separate positions of the individual institutions. The resultant depends on the individual positions and on the individual empowerments. Positions closer to the previous societal position will exercise greater power, but other positions may pull in the desired direction.

Diagram 2.3.6 illustrates a possible societal trajectory. The continuing development of the European federal state draws the UK nation along, the UK moderating but not diverting the development.

An interesting recent development has been increasing doubts outside the UK about the European project, in part associated with the current problems facing Germany. It is unclear whether this represents a temporary obstacle or a turning point in the process. Certainly such turning points are observed in other circumstances when an apparently immovable dominant force suddenly moves into a state of crisis. The collapse of communist states in Eastern Europe is one example; the collapse of the post-war consensus is another; and perhaps too we can count the sudden disappearance(?) of Thatcher(ism?) in this category.

How should these turning points be represented in the model? I'm not sure! What seems to have happened is that positions which had previously been empowering suddenly ceased to be so. This suggests that we look at the way in which the empowerment function can change. Some formulation from catastrophe theory may apply.

This completes our task of modelling the dynamics of relations between institutions. Before moving onto the next stage two points are worth noting. Firstly although the model which has been developed resembles a rational decision-making model, this appearance is deceptive — the distinction between the two models will be discussed more fully in section 3.3. Secondly whereas the model was presented in terms of two institutions and hence a two-dimensional power space, the development can easily be extended to the three-dimensional cases discussed in section 2.1 and indeed to cases involving any number of dimensions.

Diagram 2.3.5     The resultant societal position

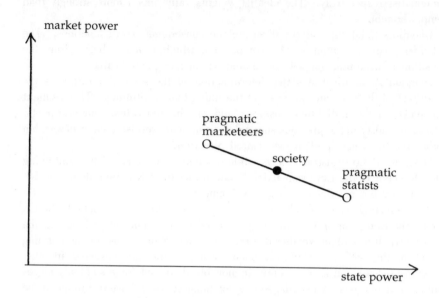

Diagram 2.3.6     The trajectory of a developing European federal state

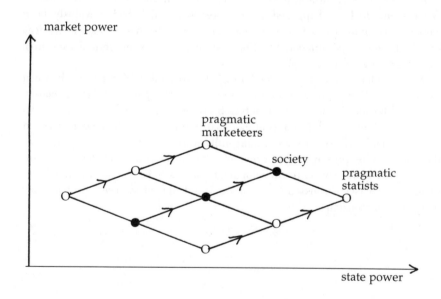

## 3. The balance of power between institutions and actors

We now turn to our second theme: the shifting balance of power between institutions and actors. Here too we can find histories of cycles in the balance of power possessing catastrophic turning points. For example the twentieth century history of Red Square in Moscow might provide a fair barometer of the power balance in Russia between people and state.

We explore this issue in three stages. The first stage concerns how institutions act on actors. The main focus will be on the rules made by institutions, and the power with which they enforce these rules and the allegiance of the actors to the rules. The power and allegiance of these rules then determine the actions taken by the actors.

In the second stage we examine how actors interact with one another within the framework of rules set by the institutions. The institutional framework which we focus on is that of the market. An alternative model of the market will be developed.

In the third stage we look at the action of actors on institutions. We focus on how rules and institutions conflict in such a way as to generate dissatisfaction with particular rules and institutions, and how this dissatisfaction leads to action against certain rules and institutions. In this way the model is completed.

### 3.1 The action of institutions on actors

So far attention has focused on institutions and their power. However these institutions do not exist in isolation. They are embedded in society. Their prime impact on society is to provide the rules which govern behaviour in society. In this section we explore how this is done. First we discuss the application of a system of rules to a space of events, yielding a system of rule domains. We then discuss how institutions influence events in two stages: first how an institution projects its rules, i.e. the process of socialisation; and secondly how adopted rules determine actions.

*Rule domains*

An example will help to illustrate the link between institutions and events in society. Consider the event of tobacco advertising in the UK. This is of concern to business, to the UK government and to the European Community. With the support of the tobacco industry the UK government seeks to resist moves in the European Community to ban tobacco advertising. If such a ban was declared we would have a situation where the rules of business and of the UK government permitted tobacco advertising whereas the rule of the European Community forbad it.

This can be represented by a Venn diagram. The whole space represents all the possible events which can happen in society. Each of the circles corresponds to those events which conform to the rules decreed by one or other of the institutions. Different regions correspond to satisfaction of different combinations of institutional rules. Thus tobacco advertising is represented by a point within two of the circles but outside the third.

<u>Diagram 3.1.1</u>        Rule domains in event space

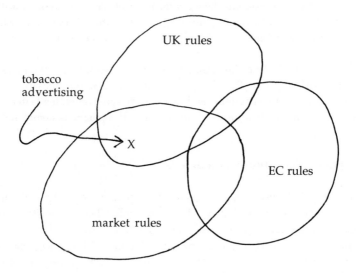

Let us now develop this model formally.

Consider events e(i) in an *event space* E.
Consider institutions I (j).
Consider rules in a rule space.
Each institution decrees a *system of rules* R(j).
Each system of rules gives rise to a *rule domain* in event space ER(j).

The domain of a rule is a region of conformity to that rule.

Events outside that region are infractions of the rule — i.e. are in the region of infraction of that rule.

Where there are two rules, there are regions of common conformity and common infraction and also regions of regulatory conflict.

If some measure can be placed on these regions then we can derive indices of common conformity, common infraction and regulatory conflict for the pair of rules.

The degree of consensus (/conflict) for the pair of rules is the measure of commonness (/conflict).

Alternatively we can take one rule as the standard measuring the *alignment* of the other rule with the standard and its *deviation* from it. Deviation itself consists of committed deviation and omitted deviation.

Where there is a system of rules, we can obtain the systemic alignment and deviation of a particular rule by combining the individual alignments and deviations of that rule with all the other rules — possibly weighting some rules more than others according to their "importance".

*Socialisation: how does an institution project its rules?*

Government propaganda, religious indoctrination and commercial advertising — they all carry strong (negative) images of a socialisation process whereby an institution projects its rules onto actors in society. In this process the institution exerts power in its attempt to make the actor both grant allegiance to the rule and concede it power.

(i) Agents
Consider a set of institutions, I(i); and a set of actors, S(j).

(ii) Situation
First we develop a concept to correspond to the initial distribution of rules. Recall that these rules are granted both allegiance and power by actors. Thus each actor has a bundle of rules, each rule carrying a certain level of power and allegiance. The power and allegiance granted by an actor j to rule r is $[\pi(r,j);$

v(r,j)]. Over all actors and rules the [ $\pi$(r,j) ; v(r,j) ] form a matrix.
So society can be represented in *actor-rules space* by the point

$$\underline{\pi v(S)} \;=\; [ \;.....\; [\; \pi(r,j) \;;\; v(r,j) \;]\;.....\;].$$

Institutions also grant allegiance and power to rules. So there is a corresponding *institution-rules space*.

### (iii) Action space

Action involves the use of power to effect change, the exercise of power having a certain "productivity". In socialisation the institution exercises power to press for a rule's adoption by an actor. Thus we can represent socialisation in terms of adoptions of rules. Societal action corresponds to a change in the societal position in "actor-rules space".

How effective an attempt at socialisation is will depend on other agents — on the receptiveness or resistance of the actor to receive this rule; and on the socialising influences of other institutions. These other institutions can either assist or obstruct the socialisation programme of the first institution. Thus one reason offered for suppressing the churches was that their socialisation programme undermined the socialisation programme of the communist state.

Therefore the resulting power and allegiance granted by the rule is the combined effect of many influences.

### (iv) Objective possibility space

### (v) Systems of meaning

Socialisation is not "just" about winning acceptance of institutional rules, it is about recruiting to a system of meaning. It is the system of meaning which generates rules and which gives sense to the rules. In major part what collapsed in the East was a system of meaning.

### (vi) Criteria

But what is it that drives the institution to engage in socialisation? The two main drivers are allegiance to the rules it is promoting and the empowerment it secures through such socialisation. Turning our attention to the European scene, what is noteworthy is the zealotry that accompanied the early stages of communism as well as the contemporary embrace of the market, or of nationalism or of religious denominations amongst those who now seek to fill the institutional vacuum left by the demise of communism.

Empowerment also follows as the allegiance of supporters propel the institution to positions of power. The allegiance of supporters also empowers through the indirect socialisation of other supporters.

In this way a socialisation process can be self-sustaining.

This suggests that the allegiances and powers associated with rules give rise to each position in actor-rule space being assigned a worth by each institution and each actor. Each agent has their own *worth function*.

## (vii) Action

Starting from the current position in actor-rules space there will be a direction of maximum increase in worth for each institution and each actor, their *worth maximising direction*, $u(i,X)$. Thus there will be a set of such directions, one for each agent. Each agent will exert power in their maximising direction. The resultant position of society will be the vector sum of the directions weighted by the powers of the actors.

$$X(t+1) = \sum \pi(i) \, u(i,X) \qquad \text{[or } em\pi?\text{]}$$

In this way the many influences discussed in section (iii) above are combined to form the resultant position.

## (viii) Consequences

This new position yields the new distribution in actor-rules space. The change is given by:

$$DX(t) = X(t+1) - X(t)$$

(This can be deduced from the socialising actions but not vice versa.)

An approximation to the value increase for each actor is:

$$Dv(i) = \sum \pi(j) \, \{ \, u(j,X) \cdot DX(t) \, \} \, v(i, u(j,X))$$

*How do rules determine events?*

Here we construct a model of how rules determine actions.

## (i) Agents

Consider the set of actors, S.

## (ii) Situation

As we noted in the preceding analysis the initial distribution of rules, registering how the rules are granted both allegiance and power by actors, each actor having a bundle of rules, can be represented in *actor-rules space*.

## (iii) Action space

Consider the *action space* of all possible actions, $\{ a(i) \}$. Societal action is the combined action of many actors — thus *societal action space* consists of multiple copies of action space, $\{ a(i,j) \}$.

Action can be conceived of in a number of ways. Here we represent action in terms of whether or not the action satisfies each rule. An action can be represented as a point in multi-dimensional space with each dimension being an indicator of whether or not the action satisfies one particular rule. The actor-action space contains multiple replicas of the action space, one for each actor. Thus the action of actor i is:

$$a(i) = [ \ ..... \ a(i,j) \ ..... \ ] \ ,$$

where $a(i,j)$ is the conformity or otherwise of the action with rule j.

Over all actors and actions the $a(i,j)$ form a matrix, $[a(i,j)]$.

So societal action can be represented in *actor-action space* by the point

$$\underline{A(S)} = [ \ ..... \ a(i,j) \ ..... \ ].$$

### (vi) Criteria

What determines whether a given action is adopted by an actor or not will depend on the power of the rule over the actor and the allegiance of the actor to the rule. (Note that this distinction is roughly comparable with Weber's distinction between coercive power and legitimate power).

In determining what action it should take each actor takes into account how the rules apply to each action; and the allegiance it gives to each of these rules and the power which each rule exercises over them. The resultant worth of each action will involve a combination of these allegiances and powers. Each actor has a *worth trade-off* which establishes this trade-off between allegiances and powers:

$$w(i) = w((v,\pi),i)$$

This trade-off worth is then applied to each action to give a *worth function* which indicates the consequent worth of each action in actor-action space: $w(a,i)$. Each actor has their own worth function.

### (vii) Action

Each actor then adopts the action which has maximum worth. Together these actions form the overall societal action. In this way the power and allegiance of rules generates a societal action.

### (viii) Consequences

Examining each action in terms of the actor's rules we can focus on the pattern of conformity and deviation by the action to the various rules. The overall *satisfaction* which the actor derives from the action will be the net amount of conformity over deviation, weighted by allegiance to each rule. Each rule is judged according as its conformity is associated with satisfaction, i.e. according to its alignment with the actor's rule system. A cumulative judgment is built up over time on this association — the alignment/deviation of the rule.

146

From each institution's viewpoint its concern is the mean conformity with its rules over society as a whole.

How does this argument relate to our discussion of European events? Consider the rise and decline of state power in Eastern Europe. State power was used against the church and the market, i.e. rules banning church and market activities were given power. This reduced the incidence of church and market actions — it rendered such actions and the institutional rules which supported them "deviationist", out of alignment with the dominant rule system. However, action was being driven by power rather than by allegiance. Once state power subsided the continuing allegiance to church and market was allowed to express itself in action. In this way the part of the model we have just developed indicates the mechanism whereby the trajectory of state power gives rise to a trajectory of popular action.

## 3.2 The interaction between actors

In the previous section we noted how institutional rules influenced the action which took place in action space. Due to our interest in whether rules were conformed to or not, we paid little attention to the nature of the actions — for example whether or not the actions were interactions with other actors. It is this aspect of interaction between actors which we focus on here. Our initial focus will be on the market. The usual model of the market tends to downplay the point, important to the argument of the present paper, that market actions conform to the rules of the market as an institution. Thus the conclusion from the previous section applies that the market institution and market rules will be judged according as they are in alignment with other rules of other institutions. Criticism from the church and others suggests that this is not always so.

*A critique of the market model*

In this section we shall explore the validity of the market model and suggest a reconceptualisation of the market, making use of the ideas developed earlier. This reconceptualisation is offered as also providing an account of interaction between actors more generally.

The central claim of advocates of the market goes something like the following:

In a market, people have the freedom to follow their interests —
in doing so they also happen to serve the interests of others —
society as a whole benefits.

In support of this claim the advocates point to the theory of the perfect market. The key features of this theory is that actors in the market-place have

147

their own bundle of goods and engage in exchanges according to market prices, rationally calculated to maximise the utility of the outcome distribution of goods.

The shortcomings of this conceptualisation are:

- failure to consider alternative formulation of the central concepts;
- failure to attend to the shaping (social construction) of some of the givens in the model;
- failure to attend to the fact that this market behaviour is socially determined by the market as a social institution — i.e. that market rules have power in society.

Let us take the first of these. The notion that each actor has their own bundle of goods tends to underplay the fact that the distribution of these goods is unequal, i.e. market power is unequally distributed. Coupled with this is the conception of the price mechanism as neutral — instead one needs to recognise that it is determination by (unequally distributed) market power. Alongside the neglect of power, utility maximisation tends to imply self-interest maximisation, neglecting other motives which do or should exist. In postulating utility functions for each actor the existence of conflicts of interests tends not to receive explicit mention. Finally rational calculation — with "perfect knowledge" — is an abstract formulation overlooking the subjectivity, the ignorance and uncertainty and the non-consequentialist nature of much choice determination.

Next consider the social shaping of some of the givens in the model. Where do the utility, the perfect knowledge and the rational calculation come from? Or rather, where do values, meanings and thought processes come from? The model makes no reference to the social construction of these.

Of course one important meaning that is socially constructed is that of the market itself. How otherwise would an actor know how to behave in a market-like way? This is a very practical question at the moment for those in Eastern Europe seeking to move towards the market — and seeking advice on what a market is and how to behave in a market.

The social construction of the market was discussed in section 3.1 in terms of the market institution having the power to ensure compliance with market rules. In general the action of institutions on actors can be thought of as the social construction of the meanings (or rules) which guide the actors' behaviour. For example the church as an institution may socially construct the givens in the market model in the following way: it constructs the utility of the bible, thus creating a market demand; it constructs a concern for others, thus somewhat diluting the maximisation of self-interest; it may construct a knowledge about social behaviour, e.g. with regards to trust, which leads to distinctive actions; and it may construct a spiritual calculus rather than a rational calculus.

Given the reservations about the market model expressed above, we now construct an alternative.

(i) Agents
Consider a set of actors, S.

(ii) Situation
First we develop a concept to correspond to the initial distribution of goods. Recall that these goods grant market power. Thus each actor has a bundle of goods of different types, each type being a source of power. The power deriving from the possession by actor i of goods of type j is $\pi(i,j)$. Over all actors and goods the $\pi(i,j)$ form a matrix, $[\pi(i,j)]$.

So society can be represented in *actor-goods power space* by the point

$$\underline{\pi(S)} = [ \ ..... \ \pi(i,j) \ ..... \ ].$$

(One might think of this space as the unfolding of the Edgworth box.)

(iii) Action space
Action involves the use of power to effect change, the exercise of power having a certain "productivity". In market exchange existing possession power is used to effect new possession power, the productivity of the action reflected in its price.

Thus we can represent market action in terms of net transfers of possessions. Societal action corresponds to a change in the societal position in "actor-goods power space".

(iv) Objective possibility space
Given an existing position in the actor-goods power space only certain positions are possible outcomes of exchange processes. We can refer to this as the *possibility surface*. The existing position is on the possibility surface corresponding to the possibility of the null exchange.

(v) Systems of meaning

(vi) Criteria
In market theory a sharp distinction is drawn between households which maximise utility and firms which maximise profit. We might think of the first as being concerned with values and the second with power. In what follows we imagine all actors being to some extent concerned about both values and power.

Each actor attaches a certain value to each position x in power space: $v(x,s(i))$. Thus each actor has a *value function*. This concept corresponds in some ways to the utility function.

We now turn to power. In the market, firms seek the power of profit. In addition to this households buy investment goods and they also buy status and fashion goods (cf. Hirsch's 'Social limits to growth'.) Thus bundles of goods are differentially empowering. So we can make use of the concept of the empowerment function developed in an earlier section.

The current position of society empowers positions in power space differentially. For example, in a society where status and fashion power exist it is more empowering for an actor to locate themselves in the fashion and of high status. Thus there is an *empowerment function* which grants power to different positions, $\text{em}\pi(x, X)$; it depends on the position concerned, $x$, and the societal position, $X(t)$.

In determining where it should position itself each actor takes into account both the value it places on that position and the power which that position will generate for themselves. The resultant worth of each position will involve a trade-off between value and empowerment. Each institution has a *worth trade-off* which establishes this trade-off. Each actor has their own worth trade-off.

$$w(i) = w((v,\text{em}\pi),i)$$

From this we obtain a *worth function* which indicates the consequent worth of each position in actor-goods power space: $w(x,i)$. Each actor has their own worth function.

### (vii) Action

Because the worth functions are defined on the full space it is also defined on the possibility surface. Starting from the current state on the possibility surface there will be a direction of maximum increase in worth for each actor, their *worth maximising direction*, $u(i,X)$. Thus there will be a set of such directions, one for each actor. Each actor will exert power in their maximising direction. The resultant position of society will be the vector sum of the directions weighted by the powers of the actors.

$$X(t+1) = \sum \pi(i) \, u(i,X) \qquad [\text{or em}\pi?]$$

### (viii) Consequences

This new position yields the new distribution in actor-goods power space, giving rise to new values of value empowerment and worth. The change is given by:

$$DX(t) = X(t+1) - X(t)$$

(This can be deduced from the exchanges but not vice versa.)

150

An approximation to the value increase for each actor is:

$$Dv(i) = \sum \pi(j) \{ u(j,X) . DX(t) \} v(i, u(j,X))$$

Again we need to ask how this relates to our discussion of the contemporary scene in Europe. In fact the final equation is highly significant. For it can be taken as being akin to the standard of living. This is something of a touchstone for the evaluation of societies. As the communist states crumbled the judgment of the Western media tended to be: communism failed because it couldn't deliver; in contrast the market economies of the West generated ever-increasing levels of prosperity to its citizens — thus demonstrating the superiority of the market. Thus in terms of the previous section market rules were in alignment with the other rules which people possessed, whereas communist rules were not. This analysis is somewhat complicated by the fact that moves towards market mechanisms in the East have provoked popular protest at the perceived threat to living standards — e.g. through increased prices and unemployment.

### 3.3 The action of actors on institutions

In the previous two sections we have looked at how institutions shape action by giving power to rules which influence actions, and at how actors interact with one another within the framework created by institutional rules. In both cases we have noted the important point that what takes place generates a judgment of the rules and their institutions — in terms of their alignment or deviation with other rules and institutions to which the actors grant allegiance.

In this section we take the argument one step further. We study the impact which these judgments of alignment or deviation have on the actors' behaviour towards the institutions. In broad terms what happens is simple enough. Alignment creates what Galbraith has recently described as a culture of contentment (a concept which quickly struck a cord with those in the UK raking over the embers of yet another election defeat for the Labour Party). Deviation creates discontent. Whether this discontent is expressed is affected by the distribution of power. That it can sometimes be expressed is attested to by scenes of popular demonstrations — which we have already alluded to.

Thus the low evaluation of a rule in terms of alignment or deviation can prompt an actor to seek changes in its institutional relationships. Actors can do this in a number of ways. Firstly actors can change their own allegiance to rules and institutions. The mechanisms for doing this are precisely those discussed in section 3.1 where we noted that an actor might resist socialisation. What is involved here is resistance ' in retrospect' . Secondly they may seek to change institutional rules. This involves the actors in a process of bottom-up socialisation — in contrast with the top-down socialisation practised by the institution. Again the same model of socialisation can be applied. Finally the

151

actor may seek to change the power of the institution. Changing the power of institutions was the subject of the model in section 2.2.

In this way actors can exert pressure on institutions. Just as we noted that the following of market and church rules was affected by the trajectory of state power in Russia, so we note that the expression of dissent has often been associated with the decline of state power as well as with the rise of dissatisfaction with the institutional rules. This completes the third stage of our analysis of the developing balance of power between institutions and actors.

## 4. Conclusion

In this paper I have tried to develop a systematic approach to the analysis of the dynamic relationship between institutions and between institutions and actors. This has involved developing a mathematical model. Although some basic terms and equations of this model have been developed there are as yet no strong ' results' . Nevertheless the qualitative features of the contemporary European history can be discussed in terms of the model — although it is worth emphasising that I have used selected events from Europe to inform the model rather than using the model to gain insight into European events.

The model does not develop any new concepts which are not already in the relevant literature. However, it attempts to fit these concepts into a much more precisely formulated model than is customary. The precision of the model offered still falls short of that which is common for economic models, but these models have theoretical shortcomings which the model here seeks to rectify. In particular I have deliberately sought to avoid rational actor models and equilibrium models, because these models contain assumptions about reality which I believe are importantly misleading.

# 11    Towards a citizen's Europe?

*Phillip Cole*

## 1. Introduction

This paper examines recent developments within the European Community and
their implications for the theory and practice of citizenship. The idea of
'citizenship' has undergone a revival in political theory. In particular, thinkers
of the left have focused upon the idea as the key to reviving socialist theory,
constituting an area of reconciliation with the currently triumphant liberal
political philosophy. For example, Geoff Andrews comments: "Citizenship
appears — in the dimensions of constitutional reform — as a historic
compromise between socialists and liberals."[1] Similarly, some on the left have
looked towards the European Community as the body which will bring about
'true' citizenship, and which will force a recalcitrant Britain to grant all of its
people 'true' citizenship rights — we will become full citizens of Europe, and
thereby full citizens within Britain. I will argue that, far from offering such hope
to the oppressed and excluded within Britain, the path the European Community
is taking threatens to add extra dimensions of oppression and exclusion.

I will examine two specific developments: the Single European Market created
by the Single European Act of 1987, which came into effect at the beginning
of 1993; and the idea of 'Union Citizenship' expressed in the Treaty of
Maastricht. For the sake of brevity I will refer to these developments together
as the EC reforms. The Single European Market aimed to realise four
'fundamental' freedoms: the freedom of movement of goods, services, capital
and persons. Under the current legislation, 'persons' refers to workers, the
self-employed, and the providers of services, and those dependent on them; the
single market is therefore concerned with those who are economically active and
their families. The notion of European citizenship offered by the single market
is therefore very thin: the primary objective of the reform is to create a single
European economy, not a single European community.

The Maastricht Treaty does provide for a deeper European Citizenship. Under

153

the provisions of that treaty, any citizens of an EC member state will have the right to stand and vote as a candidate for municipal elections and elections to the European Parliament in any other member state; and will be entitled to diplomatic protection by any Community member state when outside of the Community[2]. However, I will argue below that these particular reforms do not offer anything we can understand as a 'deep' European citizenship; and recent political developments have shown that it is the single European economy which is the priority for member states, rather than the much more divisive objective of a single political union. Therefore, I will argue, the idea of European citizenship offered by the European Community remains thin and fragmented. However, the main problem is that, even if it was more substantial, this European citizenship is built upon policies of exclusion and discrimination. It would create an increasingly hierarchical system of belonging to Europe, and an increasingly oppressive system of internal and external surveillance of those the European powers want to control and exclude.

## 2. The idea of citizenship

The idea of citizenship which left thinkers want to work with is one which goes beyond a formal or legal status, for example as defined by the 1981 British Nationality Act. One of the reasons why some left thinkers have been attracted by the European citizenship supposedly being constructed through the EC reforms is precisely because it goes beyond such formal status. I take this richer notion of citizenship to consist of belonging in a particular way to a political community, the most common form of which is the nation-state. Of course, if the integration of the European Community were to go far enough, it would constitute the relevant kind of political community. The idea of 'belonging' is more complex: it means more than the sort of 'official member-ship' I mentioned above. I take 'belonging' to a community to consist of being a member of it, in the sense of having an identity that is recognised as having a legitimate place and role to play within it, on an equal basis with all other members. The kind of membership I have in mind is that of being an equally active chooser, doer and participator within the community. The point is that one can possess formal membership of a group, but be excluded from playing an active role within it through discrimination and prejudice: full membership therefore requires equal concern and respect, and equal participation.

Having characterised citizenship as belonging to a political community, I want to distinguish between five distinct but inter-related levels of belonging:

i    *legal:*       being an equal subject before the laws of the nation state.
ii   *market:*      having equal rights to participate in the market process (e.g. as a holder of property; as a worker; as an employer).

| iii | *civil:* | having equal access to the civil rights of the nation-state; to the civil courts and tribunals of that state; and equal access to civic posts (e.g. school governorships; magistrates; etc.). |
| iv | *political:* | having equal rights to participate in the political processes of the state (e.g. having voting rights; being able to stand for political office; having political representation). |
| v | *cultural:* | having a fully recognised and respected cultural identity within the community (e.g. having a cultural identity that is shown equal respect and concern in all relevant aspects and levels of community activity). |

Each of these levels is to do with belonging to the community in a distinct but inter-related sphere of activity: and therefore each is to do with participation — in the market; in the workplace; in the civil and political processes; in culture.

These levels of belonging could be seen as hierarchical. Legal-belonging can apply to anybody who enters into the boundaries of the nation-state: they are bound by the laws of the state and also protected by them (this is not necessarily so, of course, as the treatment of migrant workers shows). But I would suggest that it is not helpful to see them as hierarchical, in that the relationships and interactions between them are so complex that any attempt to impose a rigid hierarchy upon them will break down: just because one has some degree of belonging at the political level — i.e., some political rights and a degree of political representation — it does not follow that one belongs within all the levels 'below' that.

The important point here is that one's belonging to the community can be constrained at any particular level: throughout history there are examples of certain groups being excluded from belonging to the community at particular levels — for example, people have been forbidden to own property, or to work, and therefore excluded from the market-level of belonging. Also, these levels of belonging help us to understand how a European citizenship can be constructed, and how it can be fragmented. The single-market reform extends the level of market-belonging throughout the European Community. But equally we can now see why a European citizenship which rests only upon this market-level remains thin — there are many other dimensions to citizenship which remain untouched by this particular reform.

It could be replied that the 'Union Citizenship' expressed in the Maastricht Treaty has given a significant extension to the level of political belonging, by extending the right to participate within European political processes. But the rights of political citizenship granted by the Treaty are dispersed and fragmented. Political-belonging consists in having equal rights to participate in the political processes of the political community in question. Here, the relevant community is the European Community, not individual member states of that community: having the right to vote and stand in elections of other member states does not, therefore, increase one's political-belonging to the European Community — our political belonging is simply being dispersed, not built upon. Of course, nationals of member states can also vote and stand for elections to the European Parliament, but again the right to do this in other member states does not seem to build up to the political-belonging provided by that parliamentary process. Finally, that parliamentary process itself fails to provide any significant level of political-belonging to Europe, given the European Parliament's notorious powerlessness, and the resulting 'democratic deficit' within the Community (the Council of Ministers emerged from the Maastricht Treaty as the most powerful EC institution).

## 3. Problems of belonging

It could be argued that, despite the inadequacies of the citizenship provided by the EC reforms, it is nevertheless a step in the right direction, and therefore to be welcomed. But in fact, European citizenship, however full it might become, is built upon a structure of exclusion and discrimination, and therefore presents a threat to the already precarious situation of many minority groups within Europe. The level of cultural-belonging is crucial to this argument. I described belonging to a political community as possessing an identity that is recognised as occupying a legitimate place and role within that community, on an equal basis. It is a feature of European societies that equal worth is not attached to all cultural identities, and certain groups have severe problems in belonging to the relevant political community.

The levels of belonging set out above are interdependent. The extent to which one can participate in any one is determined by the extent to which one can participate in the others: exclusion from any level has a detrimental effect on one's capacity to participate in the remaining spheres. This means, for example, that the extent to which I can be a political citizen is dependent on the extent to which I am able to participate in all the other levels of community activity. This may seem obvious in the case of exclusion from the legal and civil spheres; socialist critics would certainly make out this case with respect to the market sphere. But the fact is that exclusion from the cultural level also clearly causes problems of belonging at the other levels, and so undermines the capacity to effectively participate as a political citizen: many groups within Europe are in this precarious situation. For example, an openly gay-identified person faces extreme difficulties when standing for political office in the UK, given the homophobia inherent in the dominant British culture.

I want to suggest that we do not directly belong to the political community — we belong indirectly, through intermediary or mediating institutions. We belong to particular sub-communities, which themselves belong or fail to belong. These intermediate communities are more immediate and real for us than the overall political community, the nation-state: that is, our sense of belonging to them is stronger than our sense of belonging to the over-arching nation-state. The situation is, of course, complex, in that we can belong to more than one such sub-community, and such communities can extend across national boundaries. But by and large the political community is a community of communities, and we as individuals belong to it to the extent that the communities in which we more directly participate themselves belong. A particularly important type of mediating community is our membership of a particular *cultural* community: our sense of belonging to the overall political community depends upon whether the cultural community with which we most directly identify itself participates within that overall community.

Now it may appear that many of us do belong *directly* to the political community as individuals, in that we have unproblematic access to representation in that community. But this is because a particular cultural identity itself dominates the community at that level, occupying virtually all the important political spaces — in the case of Britain, it would be white, male, Anglo-Saxon, heterosexual identity. Others belong in a much more indirect manner, and for some their belonging to the political community is so indirect and so complex that it seems to break down altogether: members of that community are alienated from the nation-state — they cannot identify with it because it does not identify them as subjects of equal respect and concern. The central political, economic and cultural institutions are dominated by a fairly narrow cultural identity — white, Anglo-Saxon, heterosexual, male — such that other identities have problems in gaining access to fair representation within those institutions and frameworks. By 'representation' here I mean not just having representatives within those institutions, but also the way such identities are *represented* by those institutions.

The issue I want to address is that of the impact the EC reforms will have on these kinds of problems. One irony here is that belonging to Europe is highly indirect for all, which is perhaps one reason why the dominant cultural identity in Britain finds the idea of Europe so disturbing. Those whose belonging to Britain is already indirect may find the prospect of Europe far less disruptive to their identity. This is perhaps why white, Anglo-Saxon, heterosexual males such as myself are suddenly writing about issues of culture and identity, issues which black critics, for example, have been addressing for some time; and part of that process involves me and others like me appropriating the experiences, writings and ideas of those 'other' writers. But the fact remains that the experience of Europe for many minority groups has been, in Stuart Hall's words, about "exclusion, imposition and expropriation"[3]. What I will show below is that the EC reforms, rather than strengthening the position of minority groups within Europe, have made their position all the more precarious. Firstly,

European citizenship is being built upon an already discriminatory structure. Secondly, the construction of an idea of who *belongs* to Europe entails the construction of those who are to be *excluded*, and therefore a major feature of the integration of the EC member states is the sharing of techniques of control and exclusion in the construction of 'Fortress Europe'.

## 4. The European Community reforms

*Freedom of movement*

The European Community reforms aim at freedom of movement within the European Community member states. The aim is to achieve elements of the Treaty of Rome, which in 1957 demanded freedom of movement and no discrimination based on nationality for "workers of the member states". Michael Spencer[4] argues that not merely did the Treaty not specify that these 'workers' be nationals of the member states, those who drew up the Treaty intended no such restriction. However, says Spencer, EC law and policy have developed on the assumption that the Treaty *does* refer to nationals of member states, and in practice EC nationals have superior rights under Community law to non-EC nationals who live and work within the EC (between 8-10 million of them). Frances Webber comments that since 1968 Europe has operated with a two-tier workforce,

> ...whereby citizens of member states were free to travel across the Community in search of work, while guestworkers remained hostage to the 'host' community. Nor, within that country, did they have any rights worth speaking of..."[5]

Non-EC nationals, says Spencer,

> are reliant on national laws only, which in many cases relegate them to second-class status with minimal rights in such areas as protection from discrimination and access to social security, health and welfare benefits[6].

The single market reforms continue this practice, as the freedom of movement legislation only applies to EC nationals. The consequence is that:

> many long-standing UK residents (most of them citizens of Commonwealth countries) and even some categories of British citizen will not be able to move freely within the EC unless they have acquired full British citizenship"[7].

Therefore the EC reforms will create an EC-wide status from which at least one million residents of the UK will be formally excluded. We must add to this total the many more who will be unable to make use of their newly acquired EC status for economic and other reasons. Therefore the EC reforms will increase, rather than decrease, the political, social and economic stratification of British society.

Spencer's comment that some categories of British citizen will be excluded from EC freedom of movement provisions deserves expansion. The 1981 British Nationality Act formally created different levels of belonging to Britain:

i      British citizenship.

ii     British Dependent Territories Citizenship.

iii    British Overseas Citizenship.

iv    British National (Overseas).

v      British Subject.

vi     British Protected Person.

vii    Commonwealth Citizen.

viii   Citizens of Eire.

ix     EC nationals.

Only category (i) had automatic right of entry to the UK: the other classifications are more or less hierarchical in their degree of belonging to Britain. The effect of the EC reforms is that EC nationals leap-frog to second place when it comes to right of entry, over two classifications of British citizens.

The object of the 1981 Act was to bring British nationality into line with the immigration acts passed between 1962 and 1971, which had created a situation in which Britain was refusing entry to its own citizens while admitting non-citizens: many full UK citizens had no right of entry. The 1981 Nationality Act solved the problem by taking full citizenship away from those groups, who 'happened' to be predominantly black. Ann Owers comments:

> nationality law was to do with cutting down the possibility of immigration, especially black immigration. This priority meant that much of the Nationality Act merely codified and petrified British immigration law. Its provisions are dominated by a fear of who might be able to come here"[8].

But rather than simply strip UK citizenship from the former UK and Commonwealth citizens who had been deprived of entry rights under the immigration laws, the 1981 Act did give them a form of British citizenship, but a degraded form — the classifications of BDTC and BOC were created, a British citizenship that gave no right of entry to Britain. Vaughan Bevan comments:

> Whilst BDTC and BOC perpetuate, in formal terms, the UK's Commonwealth responsibilities, they are virtually meaningless in

municipal law, since they carry no right of entry into the UK. . . . They are cosmetic concepts designed to mollify local and international opinion"[9].

The EC reforms will further exclude such people, and further distance their belonging to Britain, giving superior rights of entry and residence to citizens of other EC member states.

*Internal surveillance*

The creation of 'Fortress Europe' has been noted. Jan Nederveen Pieterse says: "Europe 1992 means that, as internal borders become lower, the external borders become higher..."[10]. Another effect of the EC reforms, argues Spencer, will be increased *internal* surveillance of who is or is not 'European' and who does or does not have the right to be in Europe. If border controls disappear, says Spencer,

> There is ample evidence to suggest that unless proper safeguards are devised there will be increased harassment after 1992 of any one who is black or a member of a 'visible minority' in an EC country. Such groups already face a much higher risk than others of being stopped and searched by the police[11].

While the Metropolitan Police Special Branch opposes the abolishing of British border controls, it described to a House of Lords inquiry the steps that would have to be taken to fill the gap if they do go:

> There could well be strong pressure for the introduction of some form of nationality identity cards, extra police powers of 'stop and search', enhanced anti-terrorist legislation and more stringent registration of non-EEC nationals"[12].

A UK Immigrants Advisory Service report to a House of Lords Select Committee said of an identity card system:

> We think it *would* have the effect of increasing the sense of insecurity among black and Asian people settled in this country or visiting this country for temporary purposes"[13].

One area of likely increased harassment as part of internal surveillance of 'Britishness' is access to welfare — the welfare state has always been linked with issues of nationality and immigration. It should be noted that the British Government is currently considering the introduction of an identity card system for welfare claimants. Fiona Williams comments: "Paranoia that immigrants might scrounge from 'our welfare' was written into many of the policies of the welfare reforms of the 1920s, 1930s and 1940s"[14]. The welfare state is one site

160

of internal control

> in which entitlement to education, social security and other
> benefits and services has become increasingly dependent upon
> immigration status and in which it has become legitimate for a
> range of officials to question claimants and others about their
> status and thus act as agents of immigration control.[15]

Ruth Lister comments:

> Such insidious policies have meant a growth in the indiscriminate
> passport-checking of black claimants, all of whom are assumed to
> be a recent immigrant, even if born or long-settled in this
> country.[16]

And so if the EC reforms do bring with them increased internal surveillance to
police more severely who 'belongs' in Europe, it is members of specific minority
groups in Britain and the other EC states who will be its object.[17]

## *The Social Chapter*

The Social Charter that accompanied the EC single market reform, and the
Social Chapter of the Maastricht Treaty that further developed the Charter, have
an ambiguous status: the British Government blocked the application of the
Social Charter within the UK, and refused to have the Social Chapter included
in the version of the Maastricht Treaty which it signed, although the eleven other
member states have agreed to continue with it. But even if Britain was to
whole-heartedly adopt the ideals expressed by the Social Charter, would it take
us beyond the creation of a single European economy, towards a single European
community? While the Charter does add the 'social dimension' to the single
market, there are problems with it that lead me to suggest that despite its
presence, the EC reforms still offer a thin notion of European belonging, which
in practice is confined to the market level.

One fundamental problem is that, just as with the freedom of movement
provisions, much of the Social Charter and the Social Chapter of the Maastricht
Treaty applies to EC nationals, and would not, therefore, improve the situation
of non-EC nationals living and working within the Community.[18] They would
therefore contribute to the increased stratification of rights within the Community
member states.

Another fundamental problem that restricts the Charter's application largely
to the market level is that it is the Charter of the Fundamental Social Rights
of *Workers*. Michael Spencer points out that the words "of workers" did not
appear in previous drafts:[19] it was simply a charter of fundamental social
rights. And within the Charter's provisions, where previously it referred to
"citizens", it now refers to "workers", and, as we have seen, "workers of the

161

European Community" has been taken to refer exclusively to EC nationals. The Charter is, therefore, concerned largely with the social rights of economically active market agents, and then only with a certain group of such agents. There is nothing within the Social Chapter of the Maastricht Treaty that takes us beyond that conception: it is expressed predominantly in terms of the relationships between "management" and "labour".

The 12 basic principles of the Social Charter were:[20]

1. The right to work in the EC country of one's choice.
2. The right to a fair wage.
3. The right to improved living and working conditions.
4. The right to social protection under prevailing national systems.
5. The right to freedom of association and collective bargaining.
6. The right to vocational training.
7. The right of men and women to equal treatment.
8. The right of workers to information, consultation, and participation.
9. The right to health protection and safety at work.
10. The protection of children and adolescents.
11. The guarantee of minimum living standards for the elderly.
12. Improved social and professional integration for the disabled.

As can be seen, the majority of these principles relate to workers. Even those which may seem to have wider application are, in their detail, worker-centred. For example, principle 10, to do with the protection of children and adolescents:

> This principle sets the minimum working age at 16 and gives young people in employment the right to a fair wage, to be covered by the labour regulations which take account of their specific characteristics and also embark, after completion of statutory schooling, upon two years of vocational training.[21]

The Charter is so worker-centred because its purpose within the context of the EC reforms is to establish a 'level playing field' upon which the EC member states can compete — no member state ought to be able to gain advantage by paying low wages or allowing poor work conditions: its logic is therefore heavily market-oriented. The Social Chapter of the Maastricht Treaty has the same purpose, which is one reason why the British Government remains implacably hostile to it.

The problem is that if the Charter focuses upon our status as workers, then it does not focus fully upon our status as citizens — being an employed worker attending an identifiable workplace is neither sufficient nor necessary to our status as citizens. Firstly, as citizens we are more than just workers, and so the Charter fails to address a significant area of our concerns as citizens. Secondly, there is a vast population in Britain that does not attend an identifiable workplace, and so does not fit the traditional conception of 'worker' embodied

162

in the Charter: I have in mind here not only the unemployed who are available for work, but also home workers, carers, the retired, house-persons, children, the sick, the physically impaired — through not having access to the workplace, such people are deprived of the rights of workers at both the national and EC levels.

This is not to deny that the provisions of the Social Charter would be progressive for British workers, and is another example of the civilising effect Europe potentially has for British citizens. Angela Hadjpateras comments: "...the charter could be used as an effective weapon in the struggle for the elimination of poverty in this country".[22] However, the "heavy bias towards employment matters" means there are important gaps: "The right to social protection and an adequate income must be unequivocally extended to those *not* in employment".[23]

The Social Charter therefore works with the same market-centred logic and at the same level as the rest of the EC reforms, and so does not yet provide us with anything we can properly understand as a 'Citizen's Europe'.

## Notes

I would like to thank Roshi Naidoo for her critical contributions to this paper, and Paul Teedon for his valuable help.

1.  Geoff Andrews, Introduction to Geoff Andrews ed. *Citizenship* (Lawrence and Wishart, London 1991), p. 13. He goes on to say, "...citizenship should provide a focus for a wider engagement between socialists and liberals. An assessment of the relationship between the collective and the individual, liberty and equality, and (critically) the community and the environment is now beginning to emerge", p. 14.

2.  See David O'Keeffe, "The Free Movement of Persons and the Single Market", *European Law Review*, Volume 17, No 1, February 1992, pp. 3-19.

3.  Stuart Hall, "Cultural identity and diaspora", in Jonathan Rutherford ed. *Identity: Community, Culture, Difference* (Lawrence and Wisehart, London 1990), p. 233.

4.  Michael Spencer, *1992 And all that: civil liberties in the balance*, (Civil Liberties Trust, London 1990).

5.  Frances Webber, "From ethnocentrism to Euro-racism", in *Europe: variations on a theme of racism, Race and Class* Volume 32, Number 3, p. 12.

6.  Ibid, p. 45.

7.  Ibid, pp. 45-6.

8.  Anne Owers, *Sheep and goats: British nationality law and its effects* (Ludo

163

Press, London 1984), p. 6.

9.  Vaughan Bevan, *The development of British immigration law* (Croom Helm, London 1986), p. 129.

10. Jan Nederveen Pieterse, "Fictions of Europe", in *Europe: variations on a theme of racism, Race and Class* Volume 32, Number 3, p. 5.

11. Spencer, *1992 And all that: civil liberties in the balance*, p. 46.

12. Ibid, p. 72.

13. Ibid, p. 74.

14. Fiona Williams, *Social policy: a critical introduction* (Polity Press/ Basil Blackwell, 1989), p. 126.

15. P. Gordon, *Citizenship for some? Race and Government Policy 1979-1989*, (Runnymede Trust, 1989), pp. 7-8.

16. Ruth Lister, *The exclusive society — citizenship and the poor* (CPAG undated), p. 53.

17. For a discussion of the ways in which the European Community nation states are taking practical steps to set up mechanisms for increased internal and external surveillance, see Tony Bunyan, "Towards an authoritarian European state", in *Europe: variations on a theme of Racism, Race and Class* Volume 32, Number 3.

18. See Angela Hadjpateras, "Charting the course of poverty", *Social Work Today*, Volume 21, Number 15, December 7th, 1989.

19. Spencer, *1992 And all that: civil liberties in the balance*, p. 105.

20. Marie-Elizabeth Maës, *Building a people's Europe: 1992 and the social dimension*, (Whurr Publishers, London 1990), pp. 19-23.

21. *1992: The Social Dimension*, (Office for Official Publications of the European Communities, Luxembourg 1990), p. 84.

22. Hadjpateras, "Charting the course of poverty", p. 26.

23. Ibid, p. 26.

# 12 Evaluating international economic policies: The Cecchini Report and welfare gains and losses in the Single European Market

*Chris Allen and Frances Woolley*

## 1. Introduction

The Cecchini Report (Cecchini, 1988) and its accompanying economic report and studies (EC, 1988) represent one of the largest cost benefit analyses of international economic policy ever undertaken. In this paper we critically examine the expected economic effects of the Single European Market (SEM) and the methodology used by Cecchini to evaluate them. Our main concern is to examine why the policies result in gainers and losers and how to weight the gains against the losses. We end with a discussion of the costs of the SEM to non-European countries.

The most important elements of the SEM package[1] concern the dismantling of non-tariff barriers throughout Europe through the abolition of frontier controls, the harmonization of technical regulations, and the opening up of public procurement policies. Frontier controls are currently used to implement customs procedures, the need for which can be abolished by the harmonization of tax rates between the different countries. Domestic technical standards and regulations serve to protect consumers by imposing minimum standards and preserving health and safety controls. It is argued that these also serve to keep out foreign competitors from entering a market. It is aimed to either harmonize or abolish these. Finally public procurement, which has long been a notoriously nationalistic area is supposed to be thrown open to competition from all EC member states.

Our focus here will be on the effects of these measures on economic welfare and the distribution of income. However it is clear that the measures have other economic costs and consequences. One of the most obvious costs is the conflict between the proposals and the autonomy of national governments. The Single Market requires a convergence of national policies and preferences on a scale which may not be immediately appreciated.

The abolition of frontier controls, for instance, makes for potential conflict over taxation. A single market requires that the price of commodities all over the

165

market must be the same, else arbitrage becomes possible. This makes it impossible for any nation to have its own indirect tax policy. Clearly the objectives of nations differ in regard to different goods: the relative treatment of children's clothing and tobacco are good examples. Children's clothing is zero-rated for VAT in the UK, unlike any of our neighbours. Conversely, tobacco is taxed very highly in the UK, at least partly because it is treated as a public bad. This is obviously a very different attitude than that of the Greeks, who are producers of tobacco, and tax it very lightly.

Further conflicts may arise over mutual recognition of technical rules as Paul Geroski notes in a recent paper (Geroski, 1991). There is a contradiction between the Single Market objective of achieving large-scale enterprises which benefit from economies of scale and the desires of individual countries for their own technical standards. Perhaps the most obvious case is the German brewing industry, where large numbers of small brewers are protected by water quality laws.

The technical report on the SEM is quite explicit about what is expected to happen: "The opening up of the German [beer] market will encourage amalgamation and will also promote imports from other European countries. The likely growth in the average size of breweries in Germany should lead to an appreciable fall in production costs... Finally, once balance has been achieved, intra-Community trade could well grow appreciably, ... compared with the current negligible level of such imports. Consumers will at all events have a wider choice of products." (EC, 1988, p. 67-68). One wonders whether the average German beer drinker will share this view, when he or she suffers the loss of their local brewery!

More generally the open market will lead to a diminution of the ability of national governments to deliver on domestic public policy objectives.[2] The ability to run a full-employment economy and to influence the distribution of income (whether functional or personal) within a country will become limited in the single market. This is a point that the Cecchini Report itself concedes when it suggests in the introduction that the single market requires urgent movement towards monetary union, the idea presumably being to replace the hegemony of the Bundesbank by a more collective institution. Still, there is no necessity that nations will agree amongst themselves even within such an institution.

## 2. Welfare gains and the Cecchini methodology

The Cecchini Report estimates the welfare gains from the Single European Market at ECU 200 billion (or around £130 billion), worth some 4.5% of EC GDP (Cecchini, 1988).

There are two obvious points about this number. First of all, the gains are reduced to a single cash figure. The overall gains and losses are summed up into an overall net benefit number. No account is therefore made of the distributional consequences of the measures. This is despite the fact that the EC obviously believe that distributional issues are important, for instance, when they discuss the benefits of employment growth in relieving unemployment.

At times it appears that distributional considerations are considered irrelevant because it is believed that there will be no losers from European integration. As Lord Cockfield, the European Commissioner says of these policies in his introduction to the Cecchini Report: "[European integration is] a prospect of inflation-free growth and millions of new jobs...we all stand to gain if they succeed and to lose if they fail." (Cecchini, 1988). Unfortunately, this position is not tenable, as we discuss below.

The second point is that the number is an EC only number. Only gains to the EC itself are taken into account. Therefore, no assessment is made of the impact of the single market in non-EC countries, particularly the Third World.

Overall, the EC officials clearly foresee very substantial gains to be available from the Single Market. We can summarize these gains in three phases.

The initial phase is the direct result of the abolition of frontier controls and reduction in technical barriers. Increased competition from imports will cause an immediate reduction in domestic prices. Demand will rise and consumers will gain, but domestic producers will lose their excess profits or economic rents.

Second round effects are expected to come from increased competitiveness in the domestic market. Firms will respond to foreign competition by increasing their "X-efficiency", for example by reducing the costs of overmanning and excess inventories (EC, 1988, p. 36). The rationalization of business which is expected to take place will allow the firms remaining to benefit from economies of scale. Over time, capital stocks will be adjusted and costs will fall further as firms use a more efficient scale of production. Increased competition in traded goods will also cut firms' margins and hence reduce prices further. Cecchini treats these price reductions as a pure gain to the consumer (EC, 1988, p. 36).

Finally some of the studies, such as Smith and Venables (1988a, b), look at the situation in which all market segmentation is removed and Europe becomes literally a single market. This is an aim of the SEM, but not one which is strictly realizable given the policies implemented within the package.

The Report evaluates the result of these policies by using the concepts of consumer and producer surpluses. The consumer surplus is the area under the demand curve and above the market price (see Figure 1). This measures the difference between the consumers' willingness to pay for a good and the price actually paid. We can also define the producer surplus as the area below price and above the producer short-run supply curve. This represents the area of profits minus fixed costs (see Figure 2).

It is fairly easy to see why there is an increase in consumer and producer surplus from EC integration measures. To take the simplest case in which all imports are inputs into production, the reduction in import prices increases supply and prices will fall and output will be increased. Figure 3 shows this diagrammatically. The distribution of the gain between producer and consumer surplus will depend on the elasticity of demand. In general, both consumer and producer will gain.

## 3. Welfare gains and losses: non-Pareto improving policies

Our above example is a neatly constructed "Pareto improvement", a case in which consumers and producers *both* gain. In general, however, if there is domestic production of the commodity affected, domestic producers may actually lose out as a result of increased competition from abroad. The typical situation is shown in Diagram 2. Here we have a domestic industry competing against importers from elsewhere in the EC. D represents the domestic demand curve,

$$S_D$$

the domestic supply curve, and

$$S_M$$

the market supply curve adding domestic supply and imports.

What happens when the cost of importing falls through the Single Market? The supply of imports increases, whilst the domestic supply curve remains constant. Total market supply therefore increases to

$$S_M^I$$

and the price falls to

$$P^I.$$

Domestic consumers gain from the fall in price. Their gain will be the boxed area. Domestic output however will also fall back along the supply curve. Domestic producers will therefore lose by the extent of the shaded area. The net gain will be the consumer surplus minus this producer loss.

The *net* gain measured by Cecchini will be positive. The Commission simply take the area of consumer surplus and subtract the loss of producers. This will always be positive provided the economy is a net importer of a good. Cecchini will therefore count the overall change to be a welfare gain.

However, for the group of domestic producers, their individual loss might be considerable. It is easier to see the impact of this if we abstract from the idea

168

of self-employed people who are domestic suppliers, perhaps a group of craftspeople. The producer surplus measures their profits minus fixed costs, since it is the area between the price they get for their product and the costs of producing it. The decline in producer surplus therefore measures directly their loss of income.

In the long-run, the theory of a market economy suggests that they will find alternative jobs in other industries. But this may or may not turn out to be possible, and certainly will involve them in substantial adjustment costs.

Cases like this make it clear that the Single Market proposals do not represent a Pareto improvement; that is, not everyone is made better off without anyone being made worse off. The SEM cannot therefore be unequivocally be ranked as a welfare improvement. Some people will be made worse off.

How do economists judge policies such as these which are not Pareto improvements? Advocates of a value-free economics believe that economists simply should not make recommendations about policies which are not Pareto improvements. This effectively eliminates any role for economists in policy analysis, since any policy of any substance makes at least one person worse off.

An alternative strategy — the one adopted by the Cecchini Report — is to advocate any policy which is a "potential Pareto-improvement". Policies should be adopted if the gainers could, in principle, compensate the losers. Put in more technical terms, a policy should be adopted if the sum of the compensating variations associated with it is positive: that is, if the sum of money people would be prepared to pay in order to have the policy adopted is positive (see Blackorby and Donaldson, 1990).

There are three problems with this principle. First, the redistributive taxes required to effect this compensation do not and cannot exist. The reasons for this are obvious: the informational requirements of such taxes would be enormous and there is no way of guarding against the incentive that people would have to exaggerate their losses.

Secondly, the principle weights the social value of a monetary gain equally, no matter to whom it accrues. There is therefore an implicit ethics associated with the compensation principle. This has been noted by Blackorby (1990) who also notes in passing: "In addition, casual observation on my part suggests that it is often proponents of the Potential Pareto Principle who argue most strongly that compensation should not be paid."

Finally, there are circumstances under which, if some new policy is instituted, the gainers can more than compensate the losers; but once in the new situation, a return to the original situation could also be justified by the compensation principle. Hence the principle is not necessarily unequivocal.[3]

## 4. Evaluating welfare gains and losses.

The problem of Pareto-optimality can be overdone. There is nothing about the existing distribution of resources which is particularly optimal. Whilst the SEM is not a Pareto improvement on the existing situation, neither is the existing situation a Pareto-improvement on the distribution implied by the SEM. Some people clearly will gain, and these may or may not be precisely the people that we care most about.

The most sensible and ethically acceptable approach to welfare evaluation seems to be to state clearly who gains and loses from a policy change; and then make explicit value judgements — or a range of acceptable value judgements — concerning how we weight gains and losses.

The method of doing this in welfare economics is to utilize a social welfare function (Samuelson, 1947; Graaff, 1967). This is taken to be an additive function of individual agents' consumption. Then for small changes in benefits and costs to different individuals, we can aggregate these using the marginal social utility gains to each individual.[4]

Taking a specific social welfare function which exhibits constant relative inequality aversion, we can derive weights which are dependent on individuals' consumption relative to average consumption.[5] These are of the form:

$$a_i = \left( \frac{\overline{Y}}{Y_i} \right)^{\eta} \tag{1}$$

The coefficient $\eta$ represents the degree of relative inequality aversion. In plain terms, it tells us how the weight put upon a person's consumption falls as their consumption rises relative to other members of the society. If

$$\eta = 1$$

then the weight falls in the same proportion as relative consumption increases. Thus a person of twice average consumption would be given a weight of 1/2 a person on average income. If

$$\eta = 2$$

then their weight would only be 1/4.

The social welfare function underlying these weights exhibits a constant relative elasticity of inequality aversion. All that is important is the welfare of the person relative to the average person. This seems reasonable for an analysis which takes place at any given period of time. Of course, as time goes on and societies become richer their inequality aversion may grow (or decline!).

There are two ethical reasons why a society might be averse to inequality, each of which is associated with a particular interpretation of the coefficient $\eta$. The first argument for inequality aversion takes a utilitarian ethical position, that is, the underlying social welfare function is

$$W = \Sigma_i U_i$$

If people have diminishing marginal utilities of income, then the total amount of utility will be greater, the more equally income is distributed (Dalton, 1920). Under this interpretation $\eta$ is the elasticity of the marginal utility of income function,[6] and the higher $\eta$, the more rapidly the marginal utility of income decreases when income rises. However, as Sen (1978) notes, this interpretation leads to the paradoxical result that as

$$\eta$$

falls, the less marginal utility declines with income; hence, though the weights on inequality have fallen, the extent of inequality between different welfares has risen.

Second, we could consider the weights to arise from an explicit ethical judgement made by society as to its concern about inequality in utilities. In this case $\eta$ represents both society's weighting on utility inequality and the elasticity of the marginal utility of income.

An alternative interpretation of the distributional weights is political. Decision makers for political, ethical, or other reasons place greater weight on the income levels of certain groups in society.

How can we move from the theory of distributional weights to practical cost-benefit analysis? One approach is to observe past government decisions, and infer distributional objectives from previous behaviour (Weisbrod, 1972). Little and Mirrlees (1974, p. 240) in their book on cost-benefit analysis in developing countries confidently insist that

$$\eta$$

will lie in the range of 1 to 3 for most policy makers! Perhaps the best thing to do is to assess a range of different weights.[7]


## 5. A revised evaluation of the welfare gains from a Single Market.

In general we would like to evaluate the welfare gains from the Single Market programme, taking into account the distributional consequences. As an example of what is possible we have examined the welfare gains and losses in the 11 standard regions of the UK.

The data are taken from the Smith and Venables (1988a, b) study produced as a background to the Cecchini Report. They used an industry-level partial equilibrium models to assess the impact of market integration in the European Community in ten major industries.[8]

For the purposes of our analysis we have assumed that national product markets are already unified and that the estimated national price and output changes can be distributed proportionally to each region. Different regions differ, however, in terms of the concentration of industry production within specific regions and in terms of the initial affluence, measured by regional per capita income.

Using the constant relative inequality social welfare function discussed above, we can thus derive per capita welfare weights of the same form as Equation 1.

$$\overline{Y}$$

is taken as average UK per capita income, whilst

$$Y_i$$

is measured by per capita regional income. Relative incomes range from Northern Ireland 25% below average per capita income to the South East of England 21% above it.

The Cecchini Report treats each of these regions equally with a weight of 1 each. If we take account of inequality aversion in contrast, the relative weights of the regions varies from 0.56 in the South East to 2.4 in Northern Ireland when

$$\eta = 3.$$

The distribution of production is not uniform throughout Britain. Industries are concentrated for historic and current economic reasons in certain regions and towns. The effect of producer losses is therefore much more concentrated than those of consumer gains. For instance motor car production is heavily concentrated in the West Midlands and the South East, whilst footwear production is heavily concentrated in the West Midlands.

The footwear industry shows particularly pronounced falls in output. The UK footwear industry is relatively concentrated and protected. The reduction in non-tariff barriers in this industry particularly favours Italian firms which are much less concentrated and benefit substantially from economies of scale on a Community wide basis. Italian output increases by 72%, whilst UK output contracts by 58%. UK output also falls very substantially in the artificial fibres industry, this time to the benefit of the Germans. This makes up but a small share of UK industrial output. A more significant component is the motor car industry, which loses only 4.85 of its output, but which is far more significant in GDP terms.

172

| Table 1: Effects of Varying Inequality Aversion (£m 1985 prices) | | | | | | |
|---|---|---|---|---|---|---|
| Industry | Consumer Surplus | Producer Surplus | Net Benefit | $\eta=1$ | $\eta=2$ | $\eta=3$ |
| Cement etc. | 10.5 | -6.0 | 4.5 | 3.1 | 2.9 | 2.8 |
| Pharmaceuticals | 7.8 | 5.9 | 13.6 | 12.6 | 12.8 | 13.2 |
| Synthetic Fibres | 18.8 | -51.2 | -32.4 | -40.3 | -47.1 | -55.2 |
| Machine Tools | 6.5 | -51.3 | -44.8 | -47.5 | -50.1 | -53.4 |
| Office Machines | 35.9 | 1232.0 | 1268.3 | 1253.9 | 1266.1 | 1299.2 |
| Electric Motors | 8.5 | 0.5 | 9.0 | 8.0 | 8.2 | 8.6 |
| Household Appliances | 6.2 | -38.0 | -31.8 | -34.1 | -36.6 | -39.9 |
| Motors | 109.0 | -203.3 | -94.3 | -110.0 | -114.8 | -121.8 |
| Carpets etc. | 3.7 | -47.4 | -43.7 | -49.4 | -55.5 | -62.7 |
| Footwear | 3.1 | -293.6 | -290.6 | -311.5 | -335.4 | -362.9 |
| Total (10 inds.) | 209.9 | 548.0 | 757.98 | 684.8 | 650.6 | 628.0 |

173

We can calculate the change in producer surplus by region for each industry. We have assumed the fall in output is distributed between regions in the same proportions as industry output is shared between the regions. The change in the producer surplus is then measured absolute change in value added in the region.[9] We have neglected further input-output or multiplier effects on other industries in the region. This probably means that we have underestimated the effects; however, this is consistent with Cecchini's partial equilibrium approach to welfare evaluation.

Regional consumer benefits have been evaluated by distributing the consumer surplus calculated by Smith and Venables between regions on the basis of overall GDP size. The South East makes up some 33% of UK GDP and is therefore assessed as gaining this proportion of each gain in consumer surplus. We believe that GDP is a better estimate of effective demand than population weightings.

The overall costs and benefits are presented in Table 1. The first two columns present the (unweighted) estimated costs and benefits at £million 1985 prices for each UK industry. The third column presents the *net* benefit calculated by Cecchini, which simply sums together the unweighted costs and benefits.

Consumer surpluses are always positive, because the reduction in trade restrictions always reduces prices. Three types of overall result emerge however, depending on changes in producer surplus. In some industries, notably office machinery, both consumers and producers gain substantially. In other industries the consumer gain outweighs a small producer loss such as in Electric Motors. In other industries, notably motor cars and footwear, the consumer gain is heavily outweighed by producer loss. Overall the gain for these ten industries is positive, owing to the benefit in office machinery outweighing losses elsewhere in the industries.

How does the taking account of the degree of inequality aversion affect these calculations? Assuming that we can assess relative well-being by using per capita regional income, we can weight together the regional gains and losses using welfare weights.[10] The results for increasing inequality elasticities are shown in the other columns of Table 1

As inequality aversion increases, the overall welfare gain for the ten industries decreases considerably. This is because already deprived regions do relatively badly. The decline in welfare is particularly marked in the motor car and footwear industries. Measured welfare losses increase by some 35-30% in these industries as the elasticity of inequality aversion increases.

In principle, as the elasticity of inequality aversion increases, what was originally assessed to be an increase in social welfare could turn into a decline in social welfare if producer loss is concentrated in deprived regions. We do not find any examples of this phenomenon in any of the industries studied. However, this might have an important effect, especially as the impact on different industries is aggregated.

We have computed these estimates for the UK regions alone. In principle these calculations could and should be extended to the Community as a whole. The Cecchini welfare results are very clearly biased by the neglect of distributional issues. To give some idea of the size of the potential impact, Portugal and Greece, the poorest regions in the EC have per capita income of only 50% of the EC average. With an inequality elasticity of one this would give them per capita weights of 2 and with an elasticity of three a weight of 8.

## 6. Evaluating the effects of the SEM outside the EC

Cost benefit analysis makes two fundamental value judgements (Pearce, 1983). The first is how people's preferences are to be weighted. The previous section analyzed the sensitivity of the Cecchini Report conclusions to a range of value judgements about the weights on preferences. The second fundamental value judgements is *whose preferences* are to count. The key value judgement contained in the Cecchini Report is that the preferences of individuals outside the European Community do not matter. In this section we will explore the sensitivity of the Report's conclusions to this assumption.

The internal market measures will have a number of effects on the rest of the world outside the EC. First, as intra-EC trade costs are reduced importing countries will switch from extra-EC exporters to countries within the community. The major beneficiaries of this are likely to be the Southern countries in the EC, Spain, Portugal, and Greece. The major losers are likely to be the developing country exporters of manufactures outside the EC, who will still face high external tariffs. Koekkoek, Kuyvenhoven and Molle (1990, p. 120) estimate that the SEM will cause a once and for all reduction in import demand of $2.3 billion.

Second, economic growth in the EC triggered by economic integration will lead to an increase in demand for all goods, including imports from outside the EC. Estimates of this total trade creation effect are in the order of $9 billion for manufactured goods and $5.1 billion for primary products (reported in Koekkoek et al., p. 120).

Third, with the removal of frontier controls within the EC, countries will no longer be able to restrict or promote imports on a national basis. In certain instances, national restrictions have simply been replaced with EC restrictions; for example, the auto restrictions again Japan and the footwear restrictions on Korea and Taiwan have both shifted from a national to an EC basis, without becoming more restrictive (Winters, 1992, p. 107). In other cases, particularly for banana imports, national policies which favoured former colonies will be replaced with non-preferential EC-wide regulations, with important distributional consequences for developing nations.

Sheila Page (1990) has examined these effects for different groups of

175

developing countries. She found the impact likely to be concentrated in the Asian newly industrialized countries (NICs) and other East Asian producers. The primary commodity exporters of Africa and Latin America are expected to gain marginally because of the projected increase in world trade associated with the SEM. However, manufacturing industries in these economies are also likely to be adversely affected.

Table 2 shows the net effect of European integration on three regions, the Maghreb countries, the four Asian NICs, and the ASEAN countries,[11] as calculated by Page, and our estimates of the distributional weights corresponding to each region[12]. The distributional weights are normalized so that Europe has a distributional weight of one, that is

$$\overline{Y}$$

is equal to per capita GDP in Europe.

The striking feature of Table 2 is the sheer magnitude of the distributional weights. Even with a fairly low degree of inequality aversion ($\eta=1.0$), a dollar taken away from an ASEAN country is given 17 times the weight of dollar accruing to a European country. With a high degree of inequality aversion ($\eta=3.0$), it takes a \$4954 gain to Europe to compensate for a \$1 loss to an Asean country.

One way of interpreting these numbers is to say that the marginal utility of income in ASEAN countries is between four and 4,954 times the marginal utility of income in Europe, depending upon the assumptions we make about the shape of the utility function. Average per capita GDP in Europe is around \$15,000. Average per capita GDP in the ASEAN nations is less than \$900, primarily because of the low per capita GDP of Indonesia.[13] When incomes are lower the marginal utility of income is much higher.

| Country | Net effect (ECU m) | Distributional Weights | | | | |
|---|---|---|---|---|---|---|
| | | $\eta=.5$ | $\eta=1.0$ | $\eta=1.5$ | $\eta=2.0$ | $\eta=3.0$ |
| Maghreb | 80 | 3.16 | 10.0 | 31.5 | 100 | 995 |
| Four Asian NICs | -1491 | 1.89 | 3.6 | 6.8 | 12.8 | 46 |
| ASEAN countries | -18 | 4.13 | 17.0 | 70.4 | 291 | 4954 |

**Table 2: Distributional weights for selected developing nations**

The figures in Table 2 of course embody some heroic assumptions. The distributional weights are calculated on the basis of measured GDP in U.S. dollars. For developing countries this is a poor indication of the actual standard of living, since GDP numbers exclude much household and other non-market production, and the exchange rate used to translate national currencies into U.S. dollars may not reflect purchasing power parity.

Nevertheless, even if the figures are somewhat imprecise, they make a basic point: although the effects of the SEM on other countries may be small, from an ethical perspective we may want to weight these effects very heavily, because developing countries are relatively disadvantaged.

## 7. Evaluating the effects of the SEM outside the EC

There seem to be few convincing arguments for weighting the preferences of those outside the EC less than those inside the EC. One could argue that it is outside the power of the EC to effect the lives of those outside Europe — but that is patently false, as import restrictions and other trade policy has a clear and identifiable effect on those outside Europe. An alternative argument is that, as Europeans, we are primarily concerned with the well-being of those within Europe. This suggests taking groups of individuals who share interests in and with each other as the unit of cost benefit analysis. However, this would seem to dictate a much smaller unit of analysis than Europe — perhaps the individual European nations, or even regions within nations.

From a purely ethical perspective, an individual's nationality or place of residence does not appear a basis for concern with his or her well-being. In this paper we explored the sensitivity of the Cecchini Report's calculations to the inclusion of other nations. It turned out that, although the absolute magnitude of the gains and losses experienced by other nations was small, the distributional weight to be placed on these numbers was extremely high.

These impacts have been entirely ignored by the Cecchini analysis. The study assessed the gains and losses only within the European Community. However, this raises a fundamental problem for cost-benefit analyses, which is rarely addressed, about their general purpose and scope.

Historically, cost benefit analyses were first carried out by engineers, working out the profitability of projects for private employers. Social cost/benefit analyses today are carried out in the same spirit — a social profit/loss statement is calculated for a country or community or whoever the employer happens to be. Economists rarely question the fundamental terms of their contract — and they are rarely encouraged to do so by employers! However from an ethical perspective we cannot ignore the boundaries which are drawn around the scope of the study.

The question here concerns international distributive justice. What weight,

177

if any, do we place on the gains and losses suffered by those outside our community?

The classic treatment of international justice is provided by Charles Beitz (1979). He argues that because states are inter-dependent, the Rawlsian principles of justice apply between states. From the perspective of ideal theory, justice requires the application of Rawls' difference principle at the international level.

If the effects of European integration on developing countries will in general be negative, the implication of Beitz's argument is that we should take these welfare losses into account. Less developed countries are less advantaged than those countries in the European Community, and a loss to the least advantaged should have a greater weight than a gain to the more advantaged. Presumably what is required therefore is a similar analysis to that proposed above, but on a world-wide scale.

Were we to take Rawls' difference principle seriously, however, we might be persuaded to take a further course. It could be argued that European integration could only be justified if it improved the well being of individuals in the least advantaged developing nations. Beitz (1979, p. 174) himself argues: "the institutions of international finance and trade influence the distribution of global income and wealth and can be adapted to help compensate for the unjust inequalities that arise under the institutional status quo." From this perspective, Cecchini's Report on 1992 seems almost irrelevant!

## 8. Conclusions

The Cecchini Report on the welfare implications of the Single European Market represents one of the largest and most important cost-benefit analyses of any international economic policy. In this paper we have examined the implicit ethics embodied in the Report. The Report implicitly accepts the principle of potential Pareto-improvement, leading it to sum up the potential gains and losses into a single cash figure, purporting to measure the welfare gain from the adoption of the Single Market policies.

As a result, the Report effectively ignores any distributional consequences of the Single Market within the European Community itself. However, using the results from one of the Commission's own studies, we have shown that the Single Market will result in substantial producer welfare losses in some regions of the Community. Concern about inequality in the Community, would therefore potentially greatly revise the scale of the welfare gains expected from the Single Market.

Secondly, the Report disregards entirely the impact of the measures outside the European Community. We have again examined estimates of these effects and evaluated the potential size of importance on the basis of various ethical valuations. Again, we have found these effects to be of importance, particularly with regard to the effects on developing countries.

It is striking that the procedure adopted by the Report is at variance with almost any philosophical notion of economic welfare at all, be it utilitarian, Rawlsian, or based on some explicit judgement about inequality. It implicitly judges that inequality does not matter at all, and that welfare effects need only to be assessed within a specific geographical area.

We do not wish to press the claims of a particular ethical perspective in this paper. However, we do believe that a proper analysis of economic policy should make possible an evaluation of it from a variety of ethical viewpoints.

## Bibliographical References

Atkinson A. B. (1970): "On the Measurement of Inequality" in *Journal of Economic Theory*.

Beitz, C. R. (1979): *Political Theory and International Relations*, Princeton.

Blackorby C. (1990): "Economic Policy in a Second Best Environment" in *Canadian Journal of Economics*, 23(4), pp 748-71.

Blackorby C. and D. Donaldson (1990): "A Review Article: The Case Against the Use of the Sum of Compensating Variations in Cost Benefit Analysis" in *Canadian Journal of Economics*, 23(3), pp 471-94.

Cecchini P. (1988): *The European Challenge*, Aldershot.

Commission of the European Communities (1988a): "The Economics of 1992" *European Economy* 35, pp 1-222.

Commission of the European Communities (1988b): "Studies on the Economics of Integration" Research on the "Cost of Non-Europe", Volume 2.

Dalton H. (1920): "The Measurement of Inequality" *Economic Journal* 30.

Geroski P.A. (1991): "1992 and European Structure" in McKenzie and Venables (1991).

Graaf, J. de V. (1967): *Theoretical Welfare Economics*, Cambridge.

Hicks, J. R. (1945/46): "The Generalized Theory of Consumer Surplus" in *Review of Economic Studies* 13, pp 68-73.

Kaldor, N. (1939): "Welfare Propositions of Economics and Interpersonal Comparisons of Utility" in *Economic Journal* 49, pp 549-52.

Krugman, P. (1987): "Economic Integration in Europe: Some Conceptual Issues" in T Padoa-Schioppa (ed) *Efficiency, Stability and Equity*, Oxford.

Little, I.M.D. and J.A. Mirrlees (1974): *Project Appraisal for Developing Countries*, London.

McKenzie G. and A. Venables (1991), (eds): *The Economics of the Single European Act*, London.

Neven D.J. (1990): "EC Integration Towards 1992: Some Distributional Aspects" in *Economic Policy* 10.

Page, S. (1991): "Europe 1992: Views of the Developing Countries" in *Economic Journal* 101, pp 1553-66.

Pearce, D. W. (1983): *Cost-Benefit Analysis*, Second Edition, London: MacMillan.

Sen A. (1978): "Ethical Measurement of Inequality" reprinted in *Choice, Welfare, and Measurement*, Oxford, 1984.

Smith A. and A. Venables (1988a): "The Costs of Non-Europe", in *Chapter 5 of EC* (1988b).

Smith A. and A. Venables (1988b): "Completing the Internal Market in the European Community: Some Industry Simulations" in *European Economic Review*.

Weisbrod B. A. (1972): "Deriving an Implicit Set of Governmental Weights for Income Classes" in *Cost-Benefit Analysis: Selected Readings*, Richard Layard (ed.), Harmondsworth: Penguin Books.

**Notes**

We are grateful to Takafumi Ichimura for excellent research assistance, and to Paul Geroski and Dirk Willenbockel for comments on a previous draft of this paper. We alone are responsible for errors remaining.

1. The Single European Market, of course, is not a single policy, but rather consists of over 300 individual directives concerning everything from beer to building controls. We have followed the Cecchini report in attempting to assess the impact of the package as a whole, rather than evaluating individual items.

2. Another situation where the pursuit of national objectives, in this case environmental objectives, is seen (perhaps wrongly) as a barrier to trade is the Danish regulations requiring a wide range of products to be sold in standard, recyclable containers.

3. These are cases where the utility possibility frontiers intersect which were analyzed by Kaldor (1939) and Hicks (1945/46).

4. The social welfare function can be written as an additive separable and symmetric function of individuals' consumption $(Y_i)$. Then the social welfare function can be written as:

$$W = \Sigma_i \ U_i(Y_i)$$

We can then derive the marginal social welfare gains as a result of a policy action as:

$$\Delta W = \Sigma_i \left( \frac{\partial U}{\partial Y_i} \right) \cdot \Delta Y_i$$

where the partial derivative gives the social benefit from marginal increases in an individual's consumption. These are the weights which are put on each individual's consumption. In general they will depend on the level of the individual's income relative to other people.

5. We take a social welfare function of the form:

$$W = A + \Sigma_i \ \frac{\overline{Y}^{\eta} . Y_i^{1-\eta}}{1-\eta}$$

where $\eta$ is the elasticity of inequality aversion. Where $\eta = 1$, the social welfare function is:

$$W = A + \Sigma_i \overline{Y} \log Y_i$$

By differentiation we can find the welfare weights which are of the form:

$$\frac{\partial W}{\partial Y_i} = \left(\frac{\overline{Y}}{Y_i}\right)^{\eta}$$

which are the weights which are used for the welfare gains and losses.

6.  We take a utilitarian social welfare function, $W = \Sigma_i U_i$, and define the utility function as:

$$U_i = \frac{a Y_i^{1-\eta}}{1-\eta} \text{ or } U_i = a \log Y_i \text{ for } \eta = 1$$

We set $a = \overline{Y}^{\eta}$ in order to standardize the distributional weights to account for a country's average income levels. The distributional weights given by:

$$\frac{\partial U_i}{\partial Y_i} = \left(\frac{\overline{Y}}{Y_i}\right)^{\eta}$$

The parameter $\eta$ is the elasticity of the marginal utility of income function, $U_i' = \overline{Y}^{\eta} Y_i^{-\eta}$ (see also Pearce, 1983, p. 72).

7.  An obvious point is what such a weighting scheme misses out. Clearly the case of German beer discussed above is not covered by it. We can only measure monetary consumption and not the quality of this consumption. Sen (1978) makes the fairly obvious point that such values as liberty and justice do not enter into it.

8.  In this study, the trade between the four major EC partners was analyzed in detail, with additional blocks representing the rest of the EC and the rest of the world. Smith and Venables used the models to estimate the impact of the SEM measures on prices and output in each industry in each country. In our assessment of the producer losses we have used the long-run case of expected UK output losses in the. The long-run case arises, after market entry and exit has taken place and normal profit rates have been restored. By and large these effects are in a similar direction to the predicted short-run effects.

182

9.   We have used value added instead of profits only as used by Smith and Venables because we believe that the decline in labour income should also be included when assessing the regional impact. In the presence of high unemployment, workers will not be able to obtain other jobs. Hence the loss in labour income would not be offset by redeployment elsewhere in the economy.

10.  The formula used for the evaluation is:

$$\Delta U = \Sigma_i \left( \frac{\overline{Y_{UK}}}{Y_i} \right)^{\eta} . Pop_i \cdot \left[ \frac{Benefit_{UK}}{POP_i} . \frac{GDP_i}{GDP_{UK}} - \frac{\% \Delta Output_{UK} . Output_i}{POP_i} \right]$$

where $POP_i$ is regional population.

11.  The four Asian NICs are Taiwan, Korea, Singapore and Hong Kong. The ASEAN countries are Indonesia, Malaysia, the Philippines, Singapore, Thailand and Brunei. The Maghreb countries are Algeria, Morocco, Tunisia and Mauritania.

12.  They are calculated using national population and GDP figures taken from the UN Statistical Yearbook. All figures are for 1989 with the exception of the following GDP figures: Algeria (1988), Brunei (1984), Mauritania (1987). Figures for Taiwan not available.

13.  Indonesia had a 1989 population of 179,136 thousand, and a GDP of $US 93,966 million, making for a per capita GDP of $525.